"SPE[...]
MY
TRU[...]

Reflections on Reconciliation
& Residential School

Selected by
Shelagh Rogers
Mike DeGagné
Jonathan Dewar
Glen Lowry

Aboriginal Healing Foundation | 2012

© 2012 **Aboriginal Healing Foundation**

Scholastic Edition / First Printing

Published by: Aboriginal Healing Foundation
75 Albert Street, Suite 801, Ottawa, Ontario K1P 5E7
phone: (613) 237-4441 / toll-free: (888) 725-8886
fax: (613) 237-4442 / email: research@ahf.ca
website: www.ahf.ca

Design & Production: Glen Lowry, Anja Braun
Printed by: Hignell Book Printing, Winnipeg, MB

Printed version: ISBN 978-0-9881274-2-5
Electronic version: ISBN 978-0-9881274-3-2

"Speaking My Truth": Reflections on Reconciliation & Residential School
is the full title of this edited volume. It comprises selections from the
Aboriginal Healing Foundation's Truth and Reconciliation Series: Vol. 1 *From
Truth to Reconciliation;* Vol 2. *Response, Responsibility, and Renewal*; and
Vol 3. *Cultivating Canada.*

This project is supported in part by the Advocacy and Public Information
Program at Aboriginal Affairs and Northern Development Canada—
*Ce projet est appuyé en partie dans le cadre du Programme d'information
publique et de défense des intérêts des Affaires autochtones et
Développement du Nord Canada.*

This project was funded by the Aboriginal Healing Foundation (AHF), but the
views expressed in this reader are the personal views of the author(s).

Ce document est aussi disponible en français.

Contents

Cultivating Canada

Apologies

Shelagh Rogers

Foreword

Way back when the earth was cooling, I was an art history student at Queen's University. In part, I pursued the history of art because I am a visual learner. But it was also because art history gathered in intellectual, social and cultural history. I recall being fascinated by Paul Gauguin's 1897 painting *Where Do We Come From? What Are We? Where Are We Going?* After his experience in the then French colony of Tahiti, Gauguin returned to Europe to reflect on the violence and the beauty he had witnessed, and this painting—and the questions its title poses—remains both the beginning and endpoint of Gauguin's personal and artistic journey with truth, reconciliation, and with the very meaning of existence.

Similarly, these essays issue from the same foundational questions Gauguin asked himself. They also stem from a shared desire to renew Canada. How did we get to where we are now? Until we answer this, our future as Indigenous and non-Indigenous peoples living together is uncertain at best. *Speaking My Truth* is animated by a hope that debate—in the spirit of learning and social engagement—will take place in classrooms, reading groups, book clubs... wherever we gather to share ideas, right across this country. This book is for people who like discussion and who are energized, engaged, and jazzed by the journey of rebuilding, reconciliation, and renewal.

In sharing these stories, I hope that more of us will arrive at an understanding of our shared history and be better able to acknowledge the cold colonial spring from which Canada has come. I hope that more of us will be moved to action and that through this volume, we will deepen our self-knowledge and our empathy. History is the account we present to ourselves of our collective journey. This account, if it is to be faithful and compassionate, must include the first-hand accounts of residential school experiences. The accounts of those who were separated from their families, from their communities, and from relationships with other Canadians. Colonialism is based on an elemental violence: the taking of what is not one's to take and giving of what is not one's to give. "Where Do We Come From? What Are We? Where Are We Going?" These questions and the difficult answers they generate can no longer silence Indigenous voices.

This collection of essays delivers us to the proper work of dialogue, answering some questions but inevitably, and necessarily, provoking more. Frankly, I hope it will prod us to get off our big fat complacencies. We must investigate our own complicated histories, asking questions about the land on which we work and live. What is the history of this place? Who was here before us? How did we come to occupy and define it? What was my family's relationship to Indigenous peoples?

To answer those questions, I've been looking at my own geneal-
ogy, and I have discovered that my family is complicit in this
work of colonialism. My ancestors came from the Orkney
Islands, bringing with them the imperialism of Europe. They
worked for the Hudson Bay Company and thought that the
land was ripe for the taking. My 4x-great-grandfather was Sir
George Simpson. Having learned more about him, I now better
understand the relationship between Indigenous peoples and
the colonizers. This relationship is saddening, and it's troubling.
People like Sir George were credited with "opening up" the
country. However, when I remember that Sir George and his
contemporaries would not have been able to even survive had it
not been for the help and guidance of Indigenous peoples, who
were then often exploited by the HBC, I need to know: Why do
we not read about this in school textbooks? Why have we not yet
learned the true history of Canada? Why do we not have history
told and taught from the point of view of Aboriginal people?

The experience of reading these pieces is engaging. The variety
in this collection represents the full range of emotions, from
sorrow to joy, from anger to forgiveness. And these texts are
not without humour. Who knew that a book such as this would
contain references to singers Brenda Lee and Connie Francis (c.f.
Drew Hayden Taylor's essay)? Don't be afraid of what you will
feel as you read. It is important that you allow yourself to feel
uncomfortable. You may feel shame if your relatives were among
the colonizers. I have felt this shame. I had to witness before more
than one thousand people, at the Northern Gathering of the
Truth and Reconciliation Commission of Canada. The day set

aside for me to talk about what I'd seen, heard, and learned was July 1st—Canada Day. I felt deeply ashamed of my country and the policies that lead to residential schools. But an Ojibway elder told me that this feeling was the beginning of real learning, as rational understanding makes way for the heart to take it in. The real shame, he said, would be to feel no shame.

The longest journey is from the head to the heart. Let us open our hearts so that we may help carry the pain that Indigenous peoples in Canada, for centuries, have been carrying alone. Non-Aboriginal people will not be fully at home here as Canadians until we acknowledge the troubled genesis of Canada, its colonial past and present. When that is recognized and accepted, we will have a chance to live on this land with some feeling of wholeness and integrity.

Colonialism is not over. Its tentacles reach into the present, and it is the greatest stain on Canada. If I may quote from a publication by the The Aboriginal Healing Foundation Research Series "No other population group in Canada's history has endured such a deliberate, comprehensive, and prolonged assault on their human rights as that of Aboriginal people. Yet, despite growing recognition of past wrongs, many Canadians remain unaware of the full scope of these injustices or their impacts." And that's because colonialism has put a wall up between Aboriginal and non-Aboriginal peoples in this country. The journey from truth to reconciliation begins with hearing the stories, acknowledging our shared history (as Mr. Justice Murray Sinclair, Chair of the TRC, repeatedly states, "this is not an Aboriginal issue. It's a Canadian issue") and then setting out to fix and heal what is broken. This building and re-building will involve taking apart a whole system of colonialism and entrenched relationships—personal, political, and philosophical. In short, let's talk to each other. And let's really listen. This book is a great beginning. It isn't going to be easy, but it's our only chance. And the very soul of Canada is at stake.

Garnet Angeconeb

Speaking My Truth: The Journey to Reconciliation

When I walked into the Aboriginal Healing Foundation office in Ottawa in December 2007 to interview Garnet Angeconeb, I was unsure what to expect. I knew that Garnet was a residential school Survivor, a member of the Aboriginal Healing Foundation's board of directors, and a journalist. What I didn't know was what a warm, compassionate, and fascinating person he is. For the next two days Garnet and I talked about his life, and I felt privileged to sit with him and hear about the challenging experiences he'd survived and overcome. As I listened, I was struck by how open, honest, and generous he was in sharing his story. It was inspiring. Deeply rooted in his Anishinaabe culture and community, Garnet is an unassuming, soft-spoken, spiritual man who is passionate in his quiet and humble way. He has a vision for the future of residential school Survivors and their families and communities that he is determined to help make a reality. Garnet stressed again and again that his story is just one of many—that every residential school Survivor has a story to tell. In telling his story he made it clear that he hopes it helps others to find their voices and tell their own stories. It was an honour to work with him to bring his story to you. — Kateri Akiwenzie-Damm

At Home on Lake Seul: The Early Years

As a young child, I lived with my mother Mary, my father David, and my brothers and sister on the trapline in the Lac Seul area of northern Ontario. It was a happy time in my life. Then in 1959, when I was four years old, my older brother Harry was taken to the Pelican Indian Residential School located about twenty miles from our home. He was six years old. This was the first of many changes to occur over the next few years.

The winter of 1961 began early, and by late fall ice was already forming on the countless bays of Lac Seul. On the trapline, every minute of daylight is important. Mother and Father would rise in the wee dark hours of morning to begin their daily chores. In the evenings, I would fall asleep listening to Mother and Father talk about their day or Mother recount a story or legend. One particular night, a long turn of events began that lasted all winter. I awoke in the middle of the night and found that Mother and Father were up. My baby sister Florence and my little brother Ronald were both in deep sleep, but I sensed there was something wrong by the sound of my parents' voices.

"Your father is very ill," Mother said to me. Sitting up, I could see Father sipping tea by the wood stove, visibly uncomfortable and shaking from his illness. When I awoke again, daylight had already broken. Mother and Father were busy doing their daily tasks, only this time they seemed to be doing more than usual. Mother was packing all our worldly possessions—blankets, dishes, food, clothing, and furs. We were going back to the village of Ningewance Bay to be near help should Father's condition worsen. At least there we would be close to my grandparents, Rupert and Christina Ningewance, and their large extended families. Normally, we would have stayed on the trapline until Christmas, but not that year.

While Mother was busy packing, Father was working down by the shoreline in his *putt-putt*. "Putt-putt" was the nickname for a type of wooden boat used by the Lac Seul Anishinaabek for their commercial fishing activities in the 1960s. To keep the younger children warm, Father put a canvas shelter over the *putt-putt*, and inside he set up a little wood stove. The journey through the frozen waters of Bray Bay, where our cabin was located, to Lac Seul was slow because Father had to use an axe and an ice-chisel to break the ice in front of the boat.

At Ningewance Bay, it became clear how seriously ill my father was; he went to bed and there he stayed until the warm winds of spring arrived. Extended family members and others would help us a great deal that winter. We were so grateful whenever someone arrived with a fresh catch of fish or moose meat to feed our hungry stomachs. There were many nights we went to bed hungry and tired. Help from others was always very much appreciated.

Throughout that winter, I watched my father fade into a deep unknown illness. I was often scared. I had involuntarily become the man of the house and had to assume a lot of responsibility. I got firewood, hauled water from the waterhole down at the lake, and went for help at times when my father's condition worsened. Many nights Mother would rouse me from bed to seek help from neighbours and relatives. I would walk through the bush in the middle of a winter's night to tell people that Father was very sick and that he might die very soon. Walking along the bush trails of Keesic Bay Island with my coal oil lantern was an eerie experience. I was so scared that I never turned my head in case someone was lurking behind me. Now I realize it was probably the spirits looking after me, and certainly the Great Spirit was always watching over me. The walk home was such a relief because someone always came back with me to sit beside my ailing father.

It was a long and difficult winter for me and my family. Finally, the snow and ice began to melt. The days were getting longer. In the air there was the welcomed call of the crow—*an-deg.* The return of the *an-deg* was a sure sign of spring. Father sought help from two highly regarded Elders from the community: *Ochi-kiyashk* (Baby Seagull), otherwise known as Tom Pemmican, and *Baswewe* (Echo), otherwise known as Jean Southwind. I recall Father attending healing ceremonies with the Elders. He would faithfully take the medicines they gave to him and soon he began to feel better. Through this experience, I learned the importance of respecting Elders to the highest degree. And not only that, but to have respect for everyone. This is a lesson I still struggle with each day.

In the Anishinaabe tradition, one brings gifts and an offering of sacred tobacco to the Elders when seeking their advice. Mother and Father would gather whatever they had to take as gifts to the Elders—hunting rifles, ammunition, traps, knives, tools, or clothing. Father taught us to give things of value to others: the teaching of sharing. I also learned the importance and significance of offering tobacco. These were teachings that would help me throughout my life.

Separation: The Residential School Years

Shortly after my dad was well again, I was forced to go to the Pelican Indian Residential School where Harry was already a student. I attended the residential school and lived in the school dormitories until 1969. My older brother was there until 1968. My sister Florence was forced to go in 1968, and eventually my younger brothers Ronald and Gordon followed. Although I saw my brothers, I had no contact with my little sister because boys and girls were kept separate.

My father had attended this same residential school as a little boy. He was the ninth student enrolled when the school opened in 1927. He attended for five years. When he spoke about it, he talked only about working on the farm. The "students" were actually unpaid farm labourers—there was very little classroom teaching or instruction of any kind except, perhaps, for whatever religious teaching the children received when forced to attend chapel.

When I attended the Pelican Indian Residential School in the mid-1960s there were about two hundred and fifty of us students ranging in age from six to twelve. For six years I attended school there and lived in the dormitories. The Senior Boys Dormitory Supervisor was Leonard Hands, a young man in his early twenties. Hands came to the school from Toronto through the Anglican Church. He was not a teacher or social worker and had no qualifications for the job of dormitory supervisor. Regardless, he was given responsibility for the senior dorm that housed about forty of us boys aged ten to twelve. Hands had private quarters near the dormitory. In the morning and evening he supervised us. In the morning he made sure we got up on time, ate breakfast, did our morning chores, and attended chapel before going to the school. After school, he would make sure we did chores, had supper, attended evening chapel, and went to sleep when we were supposed to do so.

Forgetting: The Lost Years

When I left the school in 1969 at the age of twelve, I buried the memories and feelings of my time there and rarely spoke about them again until many years later. I began drinking to dull the pain and anger I felt. It was a coping method I used for a long time. I struggled with a sense of spiritual confusion and trying to figure out my place in the world.

One wickedly cold January night when I was twenty years old, I sat in a local bar wasting my paycheque on booze for me and my drinking buddies. A bunch of former residential school students sat at my table guzzling bottle after bottle of beer. One beer was not enough it seemed, yet one beer was too many for most of us.

An old school chum, Paul, screamed across the barroom, "Hey Garnet! Remember that asshole supervisor at Pelican? You know, that guy we used to call Beanie!"

"Yep! I remember that asshole! He didn't have the last name Hands for nothing. Why don't you forget about that useless piece of shit. If I ever see that bastard, I'll kill him!" I yelled back.

Once in awhile, usually while in a drunken stupor, former students would muster enough courage to talk about our negative experiences at residential school. As much as people wanted such conversations to carry on, these exchanges were always quick to end. The memories of Pelican were best forgotten and washed away by beer I thought—at least it felt like some of the pain was numbed by the alcohol.

"Paul, I've got to go," I yelled over the noisy jukebox that was blasting *Heaven's Just a Sin Away*. "I'm heading for Keesic Bay to visit my folks tonight."

I jumped on the snowmobile I had borrowed from my brother. Although I was in no shape to go, I set off at top speed into the cold winter night for Keesic Bay on the Lac Seul First Nation traditional territory where my parents lived. When I was about eight miles from home, I somehow got the snowmobile bogged down in the heavy snow around the shoreline. Try as I might, I couldn't get it out. Being a young man of twenty years, I foolishly decided to walk the rest of the eight miles. It was pitch black and the coldest night of the winter. Before long, I realized that I had strayed from the snowmobile trail. I was lost.

I had no matches to start a fire. It seemed senseless to bed down in the bush, and so I pushed on, walking out into the vast open air in the middle of the frozen lake. I quickly lost all sense of direction. I could see nothing except darkness and the snow blowing all around me. I was in the middle of a fierce blizzard, the kind of storm my father had warned me about. Each step became a real challenge as I walked aimlessly in circles in the deep slush. My boots were getting heavier as ice began to form from my knees down.

I realized that I was in big trouble. I couldn't even put my fate into the hands of the Creator. As a young person who went through the residential school system, I was deeply confused about my spirituality. I refused to believe in Jesus Christ. And now, as I lay on the frozen lake of Lac Seul, buried in the snow, I questioned how I could rely on God's help with whom I didn't have a relationship. Somehow, though, I learned to pray again that night.

After lying down half-buried in snow for what seemed like infinity, I heard the familiar sound of a snowmobile off in the distance. I looked up. The blizzard had subsided. In the dark, I could see the faint outline of the landscape and the distant flicker of two snowmobile headlights. I yelled at the top of my lungs but I was too far away. Later I learned that my father and uncle had been out looking for me.

I buried myself in snow to stay as warm as I could. I would yell every once in a while into the stillness of the night. It seemed to help with blood circulation, and I would feel warmer for a little while. It was a long night, probably the longest night of my life. Then, as I looked into the night sky, I saw a woman approaching me. She looked like my mother but it was as if she was the spirit of Mother—a holy, spiritual being. In the Anishinaabe language, the woman assured me that I was going to be all right. As she was talking to me, I noticed she was carrying a large blanket made of rabbit skins. In the sweetest voice I had ever heard, she said, "Here, I have come to cover you with this blanket so you don't get cold out here. This blanket will keep you warm."

I dozed off. By this time, I felt so warm under the cover of a loving Mother's rabbit quilt. When I awoke sometime later, I could see the early hints of the morning sunrays. It was the first day of February, my only sister's birthday. The sunrise was beautiful. The skies were beginning to glow pink and orange. I couldn't believe that I had survived that long, cold night.

I looked around me. Tobacco was sprinkled all around where I had bedded down. I unburied myself from the snow and sawed away the huge chunks of ice around my legs and feet. I stood up but quickly fell back down. I thought, now that daylight had arrived someone would soon find me. I laid down quietly to wait for help.

Help soon arrived in the form of an OPP airplane. After circling a couple of times, the airplane landed and stopped near me. Right away I recognized the two police officers who disembarked. Constable Roydon Kropp was the first officer to jump out of the airplane. He was followed by Constable Myles Lang. I was unable to walk so the two officers dragged me to the airplane. The pilot, Sergeant Larry Moore, remained on board and helped to lift me into the warm aircraft. After landing, I was taken by ambulance to the Zone Hospital in Sioux Lookout where I was laid up for three months. I had suffered severe frostbite to both feet and legs. Not only had I miraculously survived an entire night in 40° below weather, I had also escaped the real threat of amputation.

When I think back on it now, I see the vision of the woman who covered me in the rabbit fur quilt as a symbol of hope. With her loving presence, against all odds, I survived. I now know there was a reason I survived, but it took me a number of years to understand what it was.

Remembering: The Grieving Years

Understanding first began to develop on October 31ˢᵗ, 1990 when I was set on a path that I continue on to this day. I was on a business trip in Ottawa. That morning, I got up, showered, dressed, and headed downstairs to meet a colleague for breakfast in the *Toulouse* restaurant. He was already sipping his third cup of coffee by the time I got to the breakfast table.

"Hey look at this front-page article on the residential school issue," he said as he sipped his coffee.

I had my own copy of the *Globe and Mail* tucked under my arm. There, on the front page, was an article about how the then-Grand Chief of the Assembly of Manitoba Chiefs, Phil Fontaine, had publicly disclosed that he had been physically and sexually abused while attending an "Indian" residential school. As I read the article, I began to feel an indescribable pain crawling all over my body. With great difficulty I struggled to maintain my composure. I looked over to my colleague and, without thinking, asked him if he'd ever been abused while living in one of the notorious "Indian" residential schools.

His immediate response was "No." I guess I was hoping that he would say he had been. In some way I wanted him to say yes, so that we would have something in common to talk about: a legacy of abuse from the residential school system that had haunted me ever since I left the school in 1969.

I felt incredible pain build up inside me. Through this haze of pain, I struggled to admit to my colleague that I, too, like many former students, had experienced sexual and physical abuse while at residential school. I was also enraged by the psychological and spiritual scars inflicted on me and the other students from the colonialistic and genocidal approach inherent in the residential school system. My colleague and I grew almost completely silent. The silence continued as we ate our breakfast.

After a while my colleague quietly asked, "So you were abused in residential school?"

Not knowing what exactly to say, I responded, "Yes, I was abused—sexually." I told him that a man at the school named Hands, who eventually became an Anglican priest, had abused me and many others at Pelican during the 1960s. I felt a wave of rage overtake me. I had a huge lump in my throat as I struggled to hold back the pain that I had buried for so many years. Then, as if a floodgate had been thrown open, I cried uncontrollably. It was the first time I had ever told anyone that as a little boy I had been sexually abused at residential school.

For the next year I tried to figure out how to deal with that admission. I had to tell my family (I have been married since 1978 and had never spoken of the abuse to my wife). It took a lot of soul-searching—I had so many doubts. It was a very emotional time. I experienced a lot of anger and grief. My children were ten and eight years old, and I had to explain to them what was happening because my behaviour during that time was unsettling for them. I was drinking a lot and crying often. I had to come to terms with the idea of others knowing what had happened to me. I sought help from a mental health nurse who helped prepare me to meet with Leonard Hands, the man who had abused me. She made me feel validated and helped me to realize that although I'd had no control over the abuse, I did have control over the process of disclosure.

Disclosing: The Truth-Telling Years
In late 1991, I was ready. I met with Bishop James Allen of the Anglican Keewatin Diocese to disclose my abuse. The bishop

said he would come back and deal with it after Christmas. He left soon after and never did deal with it. It was very discouraging, but a new bishop, named Tom Collings, was appointed to the diocese in the new year. After discussions about an out-of-court process, Bishop Collings suggested that I meet with Leonard Hands to discuss it. I agreed. The day before my meeting with Hands, I went to the site where the abuse had taken place at Pelican Falls. Once there, I prayed for courage and strength to get me through this ugly ordeal. As I left the grounds, I spotted a bald eagle soaring way up in the clear blue sky. I took that as a sign of hope for restoration, for healing, for reconciliation, and for forgiveness.

It was April 1992 when I met face-to-face with Leonard Hands, the person who had abused me in residential school. There was strong denial from him, and the meeting ended with no resolution. Still, I realized later that confronting him was a significant milestone on my long journey toward healing.

As I pursued the matter, the first hurdle I had to overcome was denial from those around me. My parents didn't directly tell me, but did tell my siblings that perhaps I should drop what I was doing and move on with my life. Many leaders also did not support me. An Elder told me that it was because so many of them were in denial themselves. Perhaps it was too painful.

During this time I often wondered, "Is anyone out there really listening?" It saddened, frustrated, and angered me. Then I started to link up with others who were also dealing with residential school abuse. In northwestern Ontario, there was a heavy layer of silence surrounding the issue. Some people even questioned my motives for pursuing my case, suggesting that I was doing it for political gain. But as I learned about others who were taking action and began to connect with them, I began to feel supported. It gave me the strength to continue.

Still, it was very difficult. The denial and silence extended to the churches as well as the government. It took more than three years for Michael Peers, then-Primate of the Anglican Church, to respond to a letter from me, and when he did it was in a very legalistic way. Obviously, the letter was written by lawyers since the Church must have feared law suits. One of the things that I've learned, whether dealing with government or churches, is that we're afraid of each other. We're afraid to talk openly to each other.

Despite this, I continued to pursue my case. My mother never saw the end of what I started. Sadly, she died in April 1993. Later that year, in September, the OPP began investigating my allegations of sexual abuse. At first I was all alone in the allegations. By the time it was over, there were nineteen of us who had given statements about having been sexually abused by Leonard Hands. The police believed there were a lot more, and I knew myself that there were others who weren't willing to come forward. Around the same time, in 1993, there were allegations that Hands was abusing an altar boy at his parish in Kingston, Ontario. Hands was suspended by the Church, although no charges were laid. It was sickening to me to realize that he was still abusing boys, and I wondered how many others there had been in the years between.

When the police investigation of my case started, my father said that maybe I should drop it and move on with my life. It wasn't until after my father realized that two of his other sons (this meant three of his six children) were also abused by the same man that he started to change his views and became more supportive. Father also began to recognize and understand the patterns of behaviour of his sons—the anger, drinking, short tempers, and so on—that we'd been using to cope with our abuse as well as with the shame and secrecy that had surrounded it.

The sign that my father was really supportive was when he went to court on the day that Leonard Hands was being sentenced. Hands was convicted on nineteen counts of indecent assault, and my father was there in the courtroom. He realized that day that there were sixteen other men who had been abused in addition to my brothers and me. When my father showed up that day, it was one of the greatest gifts I ever received. It was a victory in the sense that I started feeling that my father was listening and that the denial had been overcome.

I'll never forget that day. It was January 5th, 1996 in Kenora District Court. I saw Leonard Hands, at last, sitting in the prisoner's box. He had pleaded guilty in court, but previous to that had vehemently denied the abuse. At the last minute he accepted a plea bargain. At the sentencing, Hands apologized to the victims of his abuse, but he specifically stated that he was not apologizing to me. He wasn't allowed to use my name but said that he was specifically excluding "G.A." from his apology. He claimed that he had already done so during our meeting in 1992 and that I had refused his apology. It angered me, but I realized he was a man going down and that it was his only way of lashing out and trying to regain some control. He received a four-year sentence. Leonard Hands was only fifty-four years old.

I rode back from Kenora with my friend, another Survivor, and we talked for the two and a half hours of the drive, so preoccupied that we ran out of gas. My friend started talking about forgiveness and I listened but at the same time I was saying, "No. I'm not ready to talk about that yet." It was not until years later that I had the urge to seek forgiveness, to forgive.[1]

Reconciling: The Journey Continues

I never received an apology from Leonard Hands. Nor did I get the opportunity to forgive him while he was still alive. I wanted to, but in the process I learned that he had died in 2000 while living at a halfway house in Winnipeg. Today, I can truly say, "Beanie (that was his nickname), I forgive you. I forgive you." I wish I could have said it to him when he was still here on this earth. Being able to forgive him has been a huge step forward in my personal healing and spiritual growth. But I know how difficult it is. It takes time and a great deal of support and love to reach that point. I hope that the

Commission can help former students, wherever we may be on our journeys, to come to terms with what happened to us at residential school and to find some peace within ourselves as we move forward in our lives.

For me, the 1998 *Statement of Reconciliation*, issued by the Honourable Jane Stewart, was another milestone in my healing process and the start of a very much needed dialogue. Some of the frustration and silence I had been experiencing lessened because I realized that people were starting to listen. I also think that because the residential school experience disrupted my relationship with my Mother, I was more receptive, and the message had more of an impact on me because it had been made by a woman.

My understanding of what *reconciliation* means has evolved since that time. To me, it's all about relationships and communication. Often, we're too afraid of each other to speak our truth openly. For me to heal, I had to find a way to do so. When I think about reconciliation now, what it means, and how it can be put into action by the Commission, I think about my friend Brian Brisket. We grew up together, went to residential school together, and were lifelong friends. In the summer of 1995, Brian and I had gone through the preliminary trial where the judge had to determine if there was enough evidence against Hands to go to court. Afterwards, Brian and I drove together on the five-hour trip from the court to Winnipeg. We talked about many things during that trip, and Brian offered me some advice: "Whatever you do," he said, "don't ever leave your family. Don't ever leave your wife and children as a result of all of this—it's not worth it."

As the case progressed, life at home became more and more difficult for me and my family. The case was taking a toll on all of us. There was a lot of tension, and eventually I reached a breaking point. In October 1995, I packed my truck and drove to the outskirts of town. I was leaving my family. I got to the Trans-Canada Highway and had to decide whether to go east or west. It was storming terribly. I made a choice, turned, and set off. I was fifty-six kilometres outside of Sioux Lookout when I encountered a horrible car accident. There were three fatalities, one was my friend Brian.

It was like a wave came over me. I felt numb, the message was so strong. Brian had told me never to leave my family and that's exactly what I was in the process of doing. After about four hours at the accident scene helping the survivors of the accident, I turned around and went home. I'm so grateful to Brian because without him, I might not have a family. I don't know what would have become of me.

Sadly, Brian didn't live to see the end of the case, to see our abuser convicted and sentenced. He never heard the 1998 *Statement of Reconciliation*. He didn't get to see the formation of the Aboriginal Healing Foundation or the Truth and Reconciliation Commission. I feel strongly that we need to remember and honour people like Brian and the many others who have passed on without seeing the steps we have taken toward achieving justice and recognition for all of the children and families who were forced to endure the residential school system. To me, that is a necessary part of reconciliation and one that the Commission can fulfill.

I believe that this Commission will provide us with an opportunity to acknowledge and validate what has happened to us as Aboriginal peoples because of the imposition of one policy enacted by the colonizing state—the policy of assimilation. The residential school policy was just one aspect of the broader assimilation policy. The overall impact of colonization and assimilation is the disempowerment of people. That is why, today, we are still plagued by issues of poverty, racism, missing women, and other horrifying impacts of that broader policy. The Commission, in some ways, can begin to turn that around so that people are empowered.

One of the things that I would like to see is a genuine apology. I would like to see the prime minister stand up along with the churches and say in no uncertain terms, "I'm sorry." If there was a collective effort to do this, can you imagine what profound rippling effects that would have? I think that a collective effort to come together to say "I'm sorry" would be very powerful.

Although the 1998 *Statement of Reconciliation* had an impact on me at the time, the statement was specific to physical and sexual abuse. It was not inclusive and did not look at the broader implications of the policy and how it fit into the government's assimilationist agenda. At the time, everyone was being very careful about what they said because of the fear of lawsuits and what any sort of admission might ultimately cost. But now is the time for us to be honest with each other. We've got to get over that fear of being sued. That is another area where I see hope for the Truth and Reconciliation Commission to instigate change. I see the Commission helping to facilitate a process of social change. A priority should be the eradication of the intergenerational impacts of residential school. My children lived with the intergenerational effects, and it is my hope that my grandchildren will not have to do so. The Commission can lay the groundwork and begin facilitating that change.

When I was young, I was afraid to speak out because it was too painful. It took a long time to have the courage to find people who would listen. I just didn't feel strong enough, I didn't have the courage to speak about something so painful that I had buried for so long. I was afraid to let those ghosts out of my system. I was afraid of not being heard so I shut it in. It would be easier today. It's in the open now so there are support systems, and more and more people are becoming aware of it and providing help. I also find a lot of courage in our Elders talking about it in ceremonies. What I've noticed is that whenever I go to ceremonies most of the Elders talk about it. They are honouring Survivors and are creating honour songs for Survivors. The role of Elders has become quite powerful. They are helping in revitalizing and restoring what was put aside and seeking that rightful place where we were before.

If the Commission can create a space that allows people to feel that their stories are accepted without fear of repercussion, perhaps it can help to neutralize some of the negativity that has poisoned our relationships with each other. When a lake is poisoned by acid rain, lime is poured in to neutralize it. Hopefully, in some ways, our relationship with Canada can be improved. It's all been so negative. I see this process as helping to lead that relationship toward the way it was meant to be. For us, the treaties were about co-existence. We need to mend those historical misunderstandings and accept the true history of this country before we can move on.

When you're ashamed of your own history, you deny—that's also what has happened on the part of the government and churches. What it all boils down to is respect. Denial is damaging and disrespectful, not healing. Our new relationships have to be built on respect.

I look at my own life and I have to ask myself, "Why did I have to go through some of those experiences?" As my own doctor said, it's amazing I'm still here. Most people would have succumbed. I look at that from a spiritual perspective and say perhaps the Creator is working through me to give a message of hope to our people about overcoming the impacts of colonization and the residential school system.

Because of those impacts, many of us went through a cultural identity crisis—loss of language, loss of family and community ties, loss of self-worth—to name only a few of the negative but real impacts of residential school. I myself lived through times of spiritual confusion. I lived through times of anger. I lived through times of cultural confusion. I lived through the disruption of my family relationships. At one time in my life, I was ashamed of my culture. To me, though, the residential school issue is not about making others feel bad or guilty. This issue is about truth and understanding. Truth and understanding are two key ingredients that will lead to healing and reconciliation.

When I look back on my life now, I can see that as a boy of six I had to walk alone through the darkness and cold and to confront my fears in order to find help for myself and my family. Then when I was twenty years old, I again had to face the darkness and cold during that long night alone on the ice. But when I felt covered by the warmth of a Mother's love, I knew I could overcome my ordeal. The process of residential school healing and reconciliation, for me, has been like that. It's amazing how strong we can be when we act out of love and respect and know we are a part of something much larger than ourselves.

May we all find the strength, warmth, and support to be able to speak our truths.

Note

1   Garnet Angeconeb, 28 March 2004, Meeting on the Future of the Residential School Healing Movement, Ottawa as reported in Castellano, M. Brant (2006:157). *Final Report of the Aboriginal Healing Foundation. Volume I: A Healing Journey: Reclaiming Wellness.* Ottawa, ON: Aboriginal Healing Foundation.

Biography

Garnet Angeconeb is an Anishinaabe originally from the Lac Seul First Nation and now living in Sioux Lookout, Ontario. After attending Pelican Indian Residential School, he completed high school in Sioux Lookout and, in 1982, graduated from the University of Western Ontario with a diploma in journalism.

Garnet worked for many years with Wawatay Native Communications Society in positions ranging from news editor to executive director. With the guidance of community members and Elders, he developed the Wawatay Radio Network with coverage to the Nishnawbe-Aski communities in northern Ontario. He also worked for CBC Radio in Thunder Bay and served as executive director of one of the northern Ontario tribal councils. In 1985, Garnet was the first Aboriginal person to be elected councillor in the town of Sioux Lookout. An active member of the Aboriginal Healing Foundation's board of directors since 1998, Garnet serves as its secretary. He is also a recipient of the Queen's Golden Jubilee Award.

In 1990, Garnet embarked upon a lifelong journey of healing, and he shares his journey with us in this collection. Garnet's story begins on Lac Seul where he lived as a young child surrounded by a loving family and concludes with his reflections on truth, understanding, healing, and reconciliation. In between, he describes how, as an adult, he struggled alone and in secret with the emotional burden ensuing from the sexual abuse he experienced in residential school. When he was ready to reveal his secret, even greater personal resources were required, but he courageously persisted in spite of the grief and anger his revelation aroused in himself and others. We follow Garnet as he confronted his abuser, first in person and later in the courts. We begin to understand how, when the time is right, forgiveness can reinforce healing and healing makes forgiveness possible. Garnet's candour, sincerity, kindness, and courage are all evident in this personal narrative of a journey from truth-telling to reconciliation.

Kateri Akiwenzie-Damm is an accomplished writer, multi-arts collaborator, publisher, Indigenous arts advocate, and communications consultant as well as an emerging video producer and director. She is an Anishinaabe of mixed ancestry from the Chippewas of Nawash First Nation in southwestern Ontario. Since 1994, she has lived and worked at Neyaashiinigmiing, Cape Croker Reserve on the Saugeen Peninsula in southwestern Ontario. Kateri worked with Garnet's written memoirs and spent hours in conversation with him to create a compelling narrative of his life.

John Amagoalik

Reconciliation or Conciliation? An Inuit Perspective

The *Merriam-Webster's Dictionary of Law* defines *reconcile* as:

1. to restore to harmony
2. to bring to resolution
3. ... reestablishing a harmonious relationship[1]

According to Dictionary.com, conciliate is defined as:

1. to overcome the distrust or hostility of; placate; win over...
2. to win or gain (goodwill, regard, or favor).
3. to make compatible ...
4. to become agreeable.[2]

Since Europeans arrived on our shores more than five hundred years ago, there has never really been a harmonious relationship between the new arrivals and the original inhabitants of North America. The history of this relationship is marked by crushing colonialism, attempted genocide, wars, massacres, theft of land and resources, broken treaties, broken promises, abuse of human rights, relocations, residential schools, and so on.

Because there has been no harmonious relationship, we have to start with *conciliation*. We have to overcome distrust and hostility, make things compatible, and become agreeable. For this to happen, from the Inuit perspective, many things need to be considered.

Canada must acknowledge its past history of shameful treatment of Aboriginal peoples. It must acknowledge its racist legacy. It should not only acknowledge these facts, but also take steps to make sure that the country's history books reflect these realities.

Non-Aboriginal Canadians cannot fully understand the crushing effect of colonialism on a people. They do not appreciate the negative self-image that people can have about themselves when another culture projects itself as being "superior" and acts to impose its laws, language, values, and culture upon the other.

Canadians must understand that their leaders had assimilation policies designed to kill Aboriginal cultures and traditions. In reference to Inuit, the *Report of the Royal Commission on Aboriginal Peoples* quoted an unnamed federal administrator as writing in a 1952 report, "Their civilization, because it is without hope of advancement, should be ruthlessly discouraged."[3] Because of this mindset, assimilation policies were implemented. Children were taken from their families and homes, placed in faraway residential schools, and forbidden to practice their languages and cultures. Aboriginal children, as young as five years, were taken from their parents and placed in schools where many were psychologically, physically, and sexually abused by church and government officials.

Some Aboriginal groups, such as the Beothuk in Newfoundland, were hunted for "sport" by white settlers until they became extinct.[4]

There are hundreds, perhaps thousands, of broken promises, broken treaties, unfulfilled obligations, and commitments. Many Canadians think these broken promises only happened in the distant past. They are still happening today. At the time of this writing (2007), the Nunavut Tunngavik Incorporated, the body that negotiated and signed the Nunavut Land Claims Agreement, is taking the Government of Canada to court because the government has not lived up to dozens of its obligations in this modern treaty, signed in 1993. It broke its past promises and is still breaking them today. The Government of Canada reneged on its commitments in the Kelowna Accord. First Nations still have to resort to highway and railway blockades, occupations, and civil disobedience to remind Canadians of broken treaties, theft, and murder.

When Inuit from Nunavik (northern Quebec) were relocated to the High Arctic[5] in the 1950s under false promises of eventual return, their human rights were violated and the Government of Canada abandoned them under harsh conditions.[6] It was decades later when the government finally admitted that they were relocated to bolster Canada's claim to sovereignty over the High Arctic Islands.[7] The Government of Canada refuses to apologize.

When thousands of Eskimo huskies were slaughtered by the RCMP, the government again pleaded innocence. They denied it happened when there is overwhelming evidence that it occurred.[8]

When Canadian sovereignty over the Arctic is mentioned today, the discussion revolves around purchasing icebreakers and offshore patrol ships without any mention of Inuit. The government seems to have forgotten that Inuit have been occupying and using the lands and resources for thousands of years. It is as if Inuit are a non-entity and not a factor in the sovereignty debate. Our use and occupancy, our land claims treaty with Canada over these lands and waters, and our commitment to Canada are lynchpins of Canadian sovereignty in the Arctic.

Martin Frobisher was recently honoured by the Canadian Mint with a commemorative coin and presented as a hero. To the Inuit of southern Baffin Island, he was a pirate,[9] a kidnapper, and a murderer.[10] He deserves no honour.[11]

Toward Conciliation

Canada needs to apologize. In order for there to be forgiveness, there has to be a genuine and sincere apology. Canada has already apologized to the Japanese and the Chinese. Why does it not do the same to the Aboriginal peoples who have been its most obvious victims over the centuries?

Canada must abandon its culture of denial when it comes to crimes against Aboriginal nations.

Canada must stop honouring historical figures who committed crimes against our people.

Canada must put in place a long-term program to improve the socio-economic status of our people, to improve health and education, and to effectively deal with the housing crisis that faces our Aboriginal communities. Canada must honour its obligations under historical and modern treaties. The legacy of broken promises must stop.

Canada must recognize and acknowledge the Inuit use and occupancy of our homeland and our commitment to Canada as the cornerstones of Canada's claim to the Arctic and its internal waters.

Zebedee Nungak, one of the foremost Inuit thinkers in Canada, has some recommendations. He writes,

> The power relationship between Canada's governmental jurisdictions and its Aboriginal Peoples has to be fundamentally corrected. That is, from a lopsided Benefactor/Beneficiary set-up, to more of a Nation-to-Nation, equal-to-equal level jurisdictional field.
>
> The country's legislatures have to deliberately make room for Aboriginal representation in mainstream political life. This includes Parliament, which, being supreme, should tackle this innovatively. Government policies towards Aboriginal Peoples have to be totally renovated. Aboriginals should not be required to go through the indignities of "surrender and extinguishment" for their lands and resources.[12]

Is There a True Commitment?

So, in order to facilitate conciliation, Canada, as a maturing nation, must take significant and sincere steps to that end. It is high time for Canada to act honourably. Looking at history, this may be asking too much.

Notes

1   *Merriam-Webster's Dictionary of Law* (1996). Retrieved 18 December 2007 from http://dictionary.lp.findlaw.com/scripts/results.pl?co=dictionary.lp.findlaw.com&topic=50/5049720b943657385f6a60f9f7123e74

2   Dictionary.com Unabridged (v1.1). Retrieved 15 November 2007 from: http://dictionary.reference.com/browse/conciliate

3   Cited in Royal Commission on Aboriginal Peoples [RCAP] (1996:458). *Report of the Royal Commission on Aboriginal Peoples, Volume 1: Looking Forward, Looking Back*. Ottawa, ON: Minister of Supply and Services Canada. The quotation is from a document entitled "The Future of the Canadian Eskimo," dated 15 May 1952 (NAC RG22, volume 254, file 40-8-1, volume 2 (1949–1952). The RCAP report continues, "The anonymous official goes on to ask what can be done about the problem of finding meaningful work for Inuit when few technicians or artisans are needed in the North. The solution, for the author, was to move the people south."

4   Budgel, Richard (1992). The Beothuks and the Newfoundland Mind. *Newfoundland Studies* 8(1):15–33.

5   In 1953 and 1955, a total of ninety-two people from sixteen families were relocated by the federal government from Inukjuaq, Quebec, and Pond Inlet on Baffin Island to the High Arctic. The author's family was among those relocated from Inukjuaq to Resolute Bay; he was five years old at the time. The Royal Commission on Aboriginal People's convened hearings on the relocation and, in 1994, it published a special report on the issue: *The High Arctic Relocation: A Report on the 1953–55 Relocation*. Ottawa, ON:

Minister of Supply and Services Canada.

6   The relocation was an ill-conceived solution that was inhumane in its design and its effects. The conception, planning, execution and continuing supervision of the relocation did not accord with Canada's then prevailing international human rights commitments. The government, in the final analysis, failed in its fiduciary responsibilities to the relocatees. An acknowledgement of the wrongs suffered by the relocatees and their families, as well as their communities, coupled with an apology is warranted.

7   The Preamble to the Nunavut Land Claims Agreement (1993) states: "AND IN RECOGNITION of the contributions of Inuit to Canada's history, identity and sovereignty in the Arctic." Retrieved 2 November 2007 from: http://www.ainc-inac .gc.ca/pr/agr/nunavut/pre_e.html

8   Inuit Elders have testified that during the 1950s and 1960s their dogs were shot by RCMP and other non-Inuit officials. This took away their ability to live independently and provide for their families through hunting, and Inuit were not consulted or offered alternatives. The killing of sled dogs was one of many acts at the time that disempowered Inuit and reinforced government control over their day-to-day lives (see "Echo

of the Last Howl," a documentary video produced by Makivik Corporation in 2004). In response, the RCMP conducted an internal review and concluded that there was no organized slaughter (Royal Canadian Mounted Police (2006). *Final Report: RCMP Review of Allegations Concerning Inuit Sled Dogs*. Ottawa, ON: RCMP. Retrieved 18 September 2007 from: http://www.rcmp-grc.gc.ca/ ccaps/reports/sled_dogs_final_e .pdf). Inuit organizations responded in a press release that disputed these findings and questioned the legitimacy of the RCMP investigating itself (Makivik Corporation and Qikiqtani Inuit Association, Joint Press Release, 5 December 2006, *RCMP self-investigation does not reveal the truth about the slaughter of Inuit sled dogs in the 1950s and 1960s*).

9   "By the year 1560, it is almost certain that Frobisher was an active privateer, and possibly also a pirate. Thereafter, all doubt vanishes." McDermott, James (2001:49). *Martin Frobisher: Elizabethan Privateer*. New Haven, CT: Yale University Press.

10 During the summer of 1577, Martin Frobisher and his crew captured an Inuk man with the intent of bringing him back to England. Shortly afterwards, some of the crew came across an Inuit encampment, and after a skirmish

in which five or six Inuit men were killed, they captured "an old woman and a younger female with a baby." The "elder woman was stripped 'to see if she were clouen footed', but was then released … The younger woman and child were secured and taken back to the pinnaces, to become the second and third of Frobisher's captives." McDermott (2001: 180–81).

11 George Best, one of Martin Frobisher's men, reported in his diary, "Having now got a woman captive for the comfort of our man, we brought them together, and every man with silence desired to behold the manner of their meeting and entertainment…"
In a book published in 1928, the author praised Best's dairy for its "remarkable account of the meeting of the two adult savages, the Englishmen looking on with interest…" McFee, William (1928:72). *Sir Martin Frobisher.* London, UK: John Lane the Bodley Head Ltd.

12 Personal correspondence with Zebedee Nungak.

Biography

John Amagoalik was born in a hunting camp near Inukjuaq, Nunavik (northern Quebec) and grew up in Resolute Bay in the High Arctic. After attending high school in Churchill, Manitoba, and Iqaluit, Nunavut, he worked as regional information officer for the Government of the Northwest Territories and then as executive director of the Inuit Claims Commission. In 1979 he was elected vice-president of Inuit Tapirisat of Canada (now Inuit Tapiriit Kanatami), and he served two terms as president during the 1980s. Throughout the 1990s, as chief commissioner of the Nunavut Implementation Commission, he worked passionately on the detailed planning required to prepare for the new Nunavut Territory. He lobbied actively for the creation of an electoral process that would guarantee gender parity in the new legislature; however, the proposal did not gain enough support to be implemented when the Nunavut Territory was created in 1999.

John has been recognized with a National Aboriginal Achievement Award, an Award of Excellence from the Canadian Public Service Agency, an honorary Ph.D. from St. Mary's University, and a Special Recognition Award from the Qikiqtani Inuit Association (QIA). In 1999, John was named a Chevalier of the French Legion of Honour. He currently works as QIA's director of Lands and Resources.

John's contribution to this collection is a clear and strong indictment of Canada's treatment of Aboriginal people in general and Inuit in particular. In *Reconciliation or Conciliation? An Inuit Perspective*, John questions whether there has ever been a truly harmonious relationship between the new arrivals and the original inhabitants of North America. He describes some of the steps Canada should take to facilitate conciliation: Canada must apologize, abandon its culture of denial, stop honouring historical figures who committed crimes against Aboriginal people, address systemic socio-economic disparities, honour its treaty obligations, and acknowledge Inuit contributions to Canadian sovereignty over the Arctic.

Inuit children who lived too far away and had to stay at school during the summer. Anglican Mission School
Aklavik, NWT, 1941
Photographer: M. Meikle
Library and Archives Canada, PA-101771
(This photo can also be found, along with many other resources, at www.wherearethechildren.ca)

Madeleine Dion Stout

A Survivor Reflects on Resilience

My father holds the reins in his hands while my mother alights from the horse-drawn wagon. I fix my red-rimmed eyes on my mother's red tam—the splash of colour, the statement, the heartbeat, the moment.

Two hours later I am fighting for dear life. The parlour is stone cold; the benches knocked wood; the windows large and paned. I beg my mother and father not to leave me. I cry until my nose bleeds. Then and there colours fade. There is nothing left to say; hearts break and moments die. I surrender the loose change I'm left with to my superiors. I buy jawbreakers and black licorice pipes for a few weeks running. Strange is how they taste.

Colonization, healing, and resilience reveal themselves to me. As Survivors, we ride waves of vulnerability for a lifetime and for generations. We were subjected to real risk factors including hunger, loneliness, ridicule, physical and sexual abuse, untimely and unseemly death. As we struggle to throw off the shackles of colonization we lean heavily toward healing, and resilience becomes our best friend.

Today, triggers continue to work on my body, mind, and spirit but, ironically, they have given me a shot at life. My mother and father hoped they would; why else would they have loosened my desperate clutch on them in the parlour? Their resilience became mine. It had come from their mothers and fathers and now must spill over to my grandchildren and their grandchildren. If we truly believe the pain of the residential school legacy has had an intergenerational impact, then it necessarily follows that there will be intergenerational Survivors too.

I firmly believe that a lot of the healing began in residential school. I have asked myself and others, did I, did we, suffer uselessly in residential school? Like any hard question I have ever posed to my mother, her answer might have been *kiýa nitãnis*, which roughly translates to "reflect on it, my daughter." The words spoken at this conference have driven me closer to home and have me reflecting on my good fortune. I have been wearing your messages like the blanket we were gifted with here.

I say that our healing began in residential school when I think of the times I lived second-hand love there. My grade four teacher, Miss Walker, spent as much time watching out the window for her RCMP boyfriend as she did watching over us students. I recall vividly her sparkling, flashing blue eyes and her pretty blue nylon blouse—the splash of colour, the statement, the heartbeat, the moment. I also well remember looking up to a window and catching an unmistakable aura of affection between a Cree woman who worked at the school and her Dene suitor. She was radiant as she beamed down on us from the window, large and paned, while he, strikingly handsome, beamed at her.

While I was deprived of love in residential school, I lived it second-hand to the fullest. Love literally filled my empty heart and soul, even though it was not rightfully mine. Second-hand love does save lives. Because of it, I can honestly say I began my healing journey in the most ungodly place. Healing is the mid-section of a continuum with colonization marking one end and resilience the other. Knowing what I know now, a large part of my response to being and becoming in an ungodly place was an act of resilience.

In the name of our best friend resilience, we can look forward to the future because we are very, very good at so many things. We are very good at wearing splashes of colour: we wear red tams as a tribute to our beloved ancestors, we display our Sundance flags, and we proudly wear our Métis sashes and our Northern prints, making a statement whether we talk "moose, geese, or fish." We are very, very good at acting in a heartbeat in the most ordinary way at the most everyday level because as Survivors we help one another do the same. We are very, very good at living the moment while marking time by preserving residential schools as monuments, producing films about them, and working together to keep important healing work going.

In the name of our best friend resilience, we must give fervent thanks to our ancestors, our beloved Elders, and our Brothers and Sisters and for all the work in the service of healing that will surely be transformative when we look back.

Thank you, *Merci*, *Hai hai*!

Biography

This is an excerpt from Madeleine's remarks on 10 July 2004 to the Aboriginal Healing Foundation's National Gathering in Edmonton, Alberta. Madeleine is an independent scholar, author, researcher, and lecturer whose distinguished career includes serving as president of the Aboriginal Nurses Association of Canada and as founding director of the Centre for Aboriginal Culture and Education at Carleton University. She is currently Vice-Chair of the Board of the newly created Mental Health Commission of Canada.

Photo: Courtesy of Janice Longboat

Fred Kelly

Confession of a Born Again Pagan (excerpt)

Father, forgive me for I have sinned.

Pity the god who made me in his image. I just turned sixty-
five and have not been to confession since 1954 at the age of
fourteen, the experience of which is clearly etched in memory. It
was an acrimonious and a deeply traumatic event in my life in
residential school. I swore I would never go back.

At that time, the confessional was an enclosed stall tucked in
the back of the chapel. It had three compartments, the central
cubicle being reserved for the priest who represented the all-
forgiving Christ. On each side was a tiny compartment where
the sinner knelt on an oak step to whisper a prepared recitation
of sins through a little screened window, following which the
deserved penance was meted out. The priest would then slide
the window shut and open the other side to hear that confession.
Usually, the penance consisted of a set of Hail Marys from the
rosary in a number commensurate with the gravity of the confession. Sins were divided into two basic categories of contraven-
tion against the prescribed doctrine: mortal sins being major

transgressions and venial sins being minor infractions. A sinner wearing a mortal sin upon death would go to hell. One carrying venial sins would go to purgatory. An unbaptized infant, presumed upon death to carry Adam's original sin from the Garden of Eden, could not enter into heaven until the final Judgment Day and would, therefore, wait in a place called "Limbo." But sins and punishment were the central preoccupations then. Such is my memory, although much seems to have changed in the Roman Catholic Church since then.

Confession is now the Sacrament of Reconciliation. The new rite may be done in three formats. The first is a celebration with one penitent. The second is a group confession, but only individual absolution is received. The third is group reconciliation where a general confession is performed and absolution is granted to all participating penitents. While the revamped sacrament still has to do with the confession of sins, the emphasis is now on healing where sinfulness is the disease and sins are its symptoms.

My confession will, more or less, follow the old protocol. It is intended for you to understand what I have gone through to get here. It will also give you my perspective on how we got to this necessary point of reconciliation. In addition, there are historical factors from the Old World thinking that have contributed to the breakdown of peace and harmony upon which Christianity, your faith, and my traditional spirituality are founded. These will be reviewed because unless we address them together, any hope of reconciliation in our society is seriously undermined.

Father, given the chance, we will come to accept what we have in common and learn to respect our differences.

How did I get here?

I was literally thrown into St. Mary's Residential School at four years of age after my father died and my mother took sick immediately thereafter. She would spend the rest of her life in and out of the hospital. My very first memory of my entry into the school is a painful flashback. For whatever reason, I am thrown into a kneeling position. My head is bashed against a wooden cupboard by the boys' supervisor. Instant shock, the nauseating smell of ether, more spanking, then numbness; sudden fear returns at the sight of the man. Was this discipline or just outright cruelty? This had never happened to me before. Where is my dad? Where is my mother? They're not here. Where are my three older brothers? Step in if they dare—they see what's happening, they watch in horror, but they are helpless. *Father, in time, that supervisor would be consecrated as a holy priest into your order.*

You and the Oblate Fathers of Mary Immaculate and the Sisters of Saint Joseph ran the school. French was always used among yourselves and the nuns who often called us "Merde cochon!" We had to learn English, it being the only language permissible among ourselves. Latin was the official language of religious rites and rituals then. Although the language was foreign to me, I quickly became proficient in Latin recitations of the Mass as a devoted altar boy. For our part, we were strictly forbidden to use our own language at any time under pain of severe punishment.

From four to seven years of age, while the other children went to their classes, my time was spent alone in the cavernous playroom. It was dark and dreary. The room seemed haunted with strange shadows dancing about in the corners. There was no kindergarten, so occasionally a playmate would be allowed to spend time with me. When she could, my mother would take me home until she had to be readmitted into the hospital. Finally, I could begin classes at seven. The first classes were spent memorizing the catechism, the manual of questions and answers that taught everything all young Catholics must know about their religion. The first question: Who made you? God made me. Second question: Why did God make you? God made me to love him, to serve him in this world, and to be happy with him in heaven forever. There were many others.

As intriguing as some of the teachings became over the years, we could never ask why the answers were as they were. To question was to doubt, a manifestation of the devil's work. To analyze was to mock God. To argue was to commit blasphemy, a mortal sin. The answers, we were told, came from God through the Pope, who was infallible. We were blessed with the true Word of God, and we were to pray for the strength to simply believe. We accepted everything, and we memorized the catechism dutifully. There was a heaven and that's where we all wanted to go, but there were gnawing thoughts always reined in by my fear of the alternative. The notion of going to hell for eternity was absolutely frightening to a six-year-old, especially one with an active imagination like mine. One day, I asked the nun who served as my teacher and catechist to explain hell.

First, she asked me about any previous burns. Every little boy knows the excruciating pain of fire. By way of comparison, she took me to the window and pointed to the thermometer outside on which the highest mark was 212 degrees Fahrenheit. She said that the sun is a million times hotter than that, and hellfire is many times hotter still. How does one not used to mathematics relate to a million? In our traditional system of counting, one million is conceptualized as running out of numbers once. That is heat beyond comprehension. If I die with a mortal sin in my soul, this is where I am going. Should I die with a venial sin, I am going to purgatory with fire as hot as hellfire except not for eternity but only until my sins have been purged. The young impressionable mind is stricken with absolute fright.

In the darkness of the dormitory and alone in bed, I am suddenly overcome by cold sweat. Although baptized into the Catholic faith, my poor unsuspecting mother still adheres to her traditional spirituality. A little boy so loves his mother that he never wants to see her hurt. Yet, in these circumstances, she is so precariously close to the door of hell. Satan will take her straight to the fires of eternal suffering never to get out once she is there. Pagans and sinners are condemned souls unless they join the faith. It's up to me. From here onward, my prayers will be perfectly sincere and ardently pious. You will never see a more dedicated altar boy offering masses served for his mother's salvation. But what about my daddy who died so suddenly? Would such a kind and loving man go to hell? If he went with a mortal sin, the answer is painfully obvious, I am told. I will never know if my prayers are too late.

My grandparents who had refused baptism because of their traditional beliefs would also be in hell for having spurned the chance to be saved. All my ancestors, for that matter, are in hell because they believed in something other than the only true Church of God. Indeed, so are all sinners and Protestants. Protestants, what are they doing there? Risking wrath but feigning innocence, I once asked in catechism class, "How do we know that ours is the one and only true faith?" My first brimstone and hellfire sermon was to follow. When she calmed down a notch, she called me to the front of the classroom where so many children had been humiliated before. "Spell the word 'Protestant'," she yelled. Her mocking tone sounded as though the word was beyond my capabilities to spell. No trouble: P-R-O-T-E-S-T-A-N-T. Now she demanded that the last three letters be struck. The naked word stood exposed. "You see, the Protestants are protesting against the true Word of God," she proclaimed loudly to make the point. Through no choice of his, one of my brothers had gone to a Protestant residential school. Was he going to hell? "Well, he's a Protestant is he not? Freddie, you just don't listen," she replied with an obvious air of vindication.

At eleven years of age, my curiosity turned into voracious reading in search of some expanded explanations perchance to reinforce my religion. Nothing was forthcoming. We moved on to grades seven and eight at a time when we were also becoming young men and women with the psychobiological changes that come with normal adolescence. More sins, but that's another story. For me, this was not an easy time. Blind faith was not doing for me what it seemed to do for others. My search became even more desperate. Outside books might do the trick. But my quest ran smack into the *Index Librorum Prohibitorum*, the Catholic List of Prohibited Books. Another priest explained that publications in the list were banned because their topics were those of heresy, moral depravity, and other matter written by atheists, agnostics, and all manner of degenerate philosophers. The List was discontinued in 1966, years after my time of desperation. The books obviously posed a danger to all of us in the faith, and this explained why no outside literature was available. We were being protected. It also explained, in part, why our personal letters to and from the school were censored. But the idea of books on philosophy tweaked my inquisitive mind even more. *Father, I sinned in coveting such books. What's more, I sneaked out of the school in search of them. I sinned again.*

We were usually confined to the school grounds and our time was regulated by a regimented schedule. On Saturdays, however, we had no classes and we might then be allowed to go into town with our parents. Otherwise, if we had the money, we might on occasion be escorted to a movie by the supervisor. Rarely did I have money. But on one memorable day, I went with the group and sneaked away during the show for a quick visit to the local library. Under no circumstances was anyone allowed to wander off alone. Breaking this rule would lead to prohibition from ever going into town again in addition to other punishment. When I arrived at the front desk, the matronly librarian pointed me to the children's section downstairs. But I told her that I was looking for the section on theology and philosophy. She smirked in bemusement. This town was known for its racism and Indians were not simply allowed to enter any public place. And what's this, an Indian kid looking for philosophy? Every aspect of her demeanour seemed condescending, but she humoured me and led me to a row of books. She bowed her head slightly to allow her glasses to slide down her nose just so far. She peered and pointed her pencil toward the section. At once my heart palpitated with fear and excitement. This time, I had gone way too far. A title jumped out at me: *Why I am not a Christian* by Bertrand Russell,[1] the renowned atheist, but of course unknown to me at the time. This book had to be mine. I stole it. *Father, I felt relieved that I was not alone after all.* Then another book struck me with awe: *Living Philosophies*, a collection of personal credos by Einstein[2] and other luminaries. There were more books on questions that had caused me so much anguish. Here was the Holy Grail. The hidden treasure was here. The library became a private and secret destination. *Father, I sinned and would knowingly continue to do so again and again. I had defied the* List of Prohibited Books. *I had now eaten of the forbidden fruit!*

Father, on the occasions we talked openly, you seemed to understand that mine was a questioning mind. Believing nevertheless that my search was evil, my only recourse was confession and prayer, more penance and contrition, then more prayers. The story of doubting Thomas, the Apostle who had to see and feel the wounds of Christ before he was convinced of the holy resurrection, rang so true to me in my predicament. The mind craved the sanctified truth of Catholicism, but there was also a compelling need to understand. My inquisitiveness did not so much need evidence as it sought plausible explanations to my perplexities. The catechism was so arbitrary, and reasoned discussions never took place. Among many others, there were questions about the Immaculate Conception. The Ascension of Christ needed at least some discussion. There appeared to be a contradiction in an all-forgiving God and his eternal punishment for a temporal sin carried at the time of death. There was a nagging question of predestination versus free will. There was unkindness and intolerance in a Church built on the teachings of Christ who had spoken on behalf of the poor, preached about understanding, and even taught acceptance of human frailties. It was also impossible for me to accept that my ancestors, who had not known about the religion prior to the arrival of the missionaries, could be condemned to hell for not following the Catholic way of life. I was told that these were some of the mysteries that one must simply accept as part of salvation. But by natural disposition, I was not easily given to blind faith.

At fourteen and going into grade nine, I went through what all Catholic boys must go through at one time or another. *Your dedication and apparent peace of mind was an inspiration. Father, the priesthood seemed attractive.* Here the answers and my life's work would surely be found. With great surprise, my application to enter the seminary was accepted. But something happened on the way to my Damascus.

Questions about my religion persisted and constituted the most oft-repeated recitations in the confessional. So monotonously recurrent must my sins have become that the priest in the confessional that day finally stirred from his usually passive composure and asked impatiently if this was Freddie. "Yes," I replied with surprise and nervousness. He admonished sternly, "Why don't you get these doubts out of your head and be a good Catholic boy like you're supposed to be." The forgiving Christ, represented by the priest, suddenly became a scowling human being, indeed a very intense, scolding old man. In the classroom, the use of the name "Freddie" was usually followed by a painful clout to the ears, a deafening shock to the eardrums that left a burning sensation and a lingering hum fading into a distant buzz. My reaction was impulsive and my words came out in a quick defiant whisper: "If I were a good Catholic boy, I wouldn't be here." Outside the confessional, this priest doubled as the principal of the school. I was in very deep trouble. "Don't talk back," snapped my confessor. "Well, don't give me hell," I blurted unaware of my prophetic words. This was a sacrilege, an act of unforgivable irreverence to Christ, the confessional, the sacrament, the priest, and everything the Church stood for. Stunned by my own insolence, I arose and slithered out of the confessional like the condemned serpent banished from the Garden of Eden. I was certain of only one thing, excommunication from the Church leading to eternal damnation. Stepping back into the chapel, the altar bells rang as the chalice was raised in consecration, the most sacred part of the Mass. But instead of all heads bowed in reverence as the wine was being transformed into the blood of Christ, the whole congregation, so it seemed, was turned back toward our commotion in the confessional. This would be my last time in the confessional, although I continued to attend religious ceremonies in this state of mortal sin for the rest of my years in residential school, thus compounding my damnation. *This was surely the time to leave school. I no longer belonged here, and I was certain that I no longer belonged in the faith. Yet, Father, I was transferred to another residential school even further from home. I was sent from St. Mary's in Kenora, Ontario, to St.Paul's High in Lebret, Saskatchewan.*

The Residential School System
Father, I have already made reference to the complicity between the churches and the government. To borrow some sentiment of the times, there were still many wretched souls to be converted and, if the Indians could not be exterminated, many more would be born.

From 1831 to 1998, residential schools into which Indian children were forcibly placed operated across Canada.[9] The churches would run these schools. At first the schools were located near reserves, but by 1900, it became evident that the policy of assimilation was not working. The children had to be taken away from the pagan influence of their parents. Changes to the *Indian Act* enabled the schools to relocate away from reserves, which they did. Further legislative changes to the *Indian Act* in 1920 allowed for children between the ages of seven and fifteen to be forcibly removed from their parents and placed into these schools. Some families withdrew into their traditional territories to keep their children away from the churches and the school. It then became punishable by law, not only for the children to be out of school, but also for parents to withhold children from attending these schools.

Restrictions on their civil rights meant that "Indians" were not "persons" under the law and therefore had no means of challenging intrusions on their families and communities. For all intents and purposes Indians were considered to be "wards of the government," and this made it possible and easy for churches to assume legal custody of Indian children in the residential schools. Thus, care and treatment of the children were at the total and unquestioned discretion of the churches and their personnel.

Many changes over the years reflected the various attempts to force assimilation upon us. No amount of brainwashing and punishment had the desired effect of beating the savagery out of us heathens. Certainly there was serious and irreversible damage, but no policy could assimilate us.

Immediately upon entry into the school, the staff began to beat the devil out of us. Such was my experience. We were humiliated out of our culture and spirituality. We were told that these ways were of the devil. We were punished for speaking the only language we ever knew. Fear stalked the dark halls of the school as priests and nuns going about their rounds in black robes passed like floating shadows in the night. Crying from fear was punished by beatings that brought on more crying and then more punishment. Braids were immediately shorn. Traditional clothing was confiscated and replaced by standard issue uniforms. Our traditional names were anglicized and often replaced by numbers. Those who ran away were held in dark closets and fed a bread-and-water diet when they were brought back. Any sense of dignity and self-esteem turned to self-worthlessness and hopelessness. We came to believe that "Indian" was a dirty word, oftentimes calling each other by that term pejoratively. Many of us were physically beaten, sexually fondled, molested, and raped.

The future seemed hopeless. We were incarcerated for no other reason than being Indian. We were deprived of the care, love, and guidance of our parents during our most critical years of childhood. The time we could have learned the critical parenting skills and values was lost to the generations that attended residential schools, the effects of which still haunt us and will continue to have impacts upon our people and communities. In many instances, our role models were the same priests and nuns who were our sexual predators and perpetrators. To be absolutely certain, not all the religious staff committed such sexual atrocities. To their credit, many appeared pure and conscientious in their duties. But having taken their vows of lifelong chastity and celibacy, and even giving them the benefit of any doubt, they were understandably hard-pressed to talk about the act of procreation, personal parenting, and other normal facts of life in a Church that taught us that sex was a taboo subject in school. In fact, there was no such thing as a healthy sex education. Sex was dirty, and even thoughts about sex were sins—matters, indeed, for the confessional. Touching a girl in any way would lead ultimately to "one dirty act," said the nuns invariably. Once planted in the mind during the formative years of an adolescent boy, this notion was insidiously inescapable, even sounding implausible. The psychological damage was done. Many fathers to this day are unable to express their love to their children, especially their daughters. Personally, I was not able to hug or kiss my mother until she was seventy-three, the final year of her life.

Father, I tried to rationalize what I saw and experienced. The treatment of children, as horrific as it was, must have been our normal lot for having been the pagan sinners that we had been. Was everything all right? Was it even humane? None of us had any idea as to what the law was regarding children but somehow there was a general feeling that it did not apply to us anyway. Even the crown attorney from town was in the chapel for Mass every Sunday. So things must have been all right, not known, or condoned. Besides, we were afraid to say anything to anyone outside the school. Would anybody believe us anyway? If we told our parents, and they came to our rescue, the police would be called to arrest them. If that were not enough, we were told that violence committed or intended against a person of the cloth was an unforgivable sin deserving of immediate condemnation into hell, but it seemed permissible for them to touch us. Those students who were sexually abused suffered a trauma so severe that it affected them, not only then, but also for the rest of their lives. Uncomfortable as it was, we kept quiet. We would abide the unwritten code among the students: never rat.

Because I came to hate everyone connected to the school and the religion—the nuns, priests, brothers, and the staff—I

committed a sin. For that, I repent. And for the times I blamed
God for the pain and anguish that we were going through and
allowed myself to think in anger that he was mean and wicked,
I sinned against him. I am deeply remorseful. For all the things
that I personally saw and experienced and knew were wrong
but did not report to the authorities, I committed an act of
complicity. To all the students in residential schools who were
with me and have now passed on, I sincerely regret that I did
not fight harder at the time.

Would this nightmare ever end? Finally, after over one hundred
and sixty years, the actual nightmare ended. In 1998, the last
residential school was shut down, but the aftershocks continue.

My Personal Reconciliation

Father, I have shared much with you that needed to be said.
Respectfully, I am not seeking penance and far be it for me to
deny hell. I have seen it. It is here and it is man-made. Forgive
me if you must and pray for me. But it is reconciliation that I
seek—between you and me and our respective peoples. We need
to build a new future. You have also glimpsed into my own
reconciliation, the note upon which we should leave for now.

Personal reconciliation is making peace with one's own self and
reclaiming one's identity. Through the kindness of the Creator,
I am at peace with myself. I have returned to Midewewin, the
principal spirituality of the Anishinaabe. I have come to under-
stand and respect the interconnectedness of all life, and I am

very happy with my place in creation, humble as it is. Mine are the gifts of life so sacredly conferred upon my ancestors by the Creator. Through this spirituality, mine also are the experiences that have rendered insights into life's eternal questions: whence, what, whither, and why.

I am contentedly reconciled to traditional spirituality as my living philosophy. Now, mine is an unconditional wish to reach out and help people on the basis of my culture and traditional ways. I have received the honour of being referred to as an Elder, a custodian of traditions, customs, laws, and spirituality. May I be forever worthy of those who wish to claim the traditional teachings that are theirs through me and other elders. May I continue to be deserving of the privilege of receiving youth who seek strength, courage, and enlightenment through my ceremonies. Having nothing to teach you but much to share, I reach out to you also and the other players in the legacy of the residential schools.

A government founded on peace, order, and good government and yet responsible for inflicting the horror of the residential school system is one that I am prepared to meet with to discuss the rule of law that includes enforcement of Aboriginal rights and treaties as the basis for a reconciled future. A church that validated the ruthless superiority complex of European monarchs to persecute Indigenous people, steal their land, and overrun their cultures by condemning them as ways of the devil is one I am also prepared to discuss reconciliation with. My willingness to do this is based on having sincere regard for the seven traditional laws of Creation. A clergy abiding a faith founded on the teachings of Christ, who so loved the purity and innocence of children, yet whose own agents inflicted sexual and physical abuse on Aboriginal children are men and women I am prepared to meet in my community to discuss reconciliation. And should they still believe in hell, may they be spared. Yes, Father, I am prepared.

In ultimate personal reaffirmation, it was not God that hurt generations of innocent children, but the human beings in the churches who undertook to deliver Christianity and inflicted the sorrow in His name. It is not my right or prerogative to forgive what was done to my brothers, my sisters, and my dearest friends as they must speak for themselves and, unfortunately, many of them are now dead. Nevertheless, I dedicate this statement of reconciliation to their memory. I can speak for myself, Father. I am happy that my ancestors saw fit to bring their sacred beliefs underground when they were banned and persecuted. Because of them and the Creator, the ways of my people are alive and in them I have found my answers.

I gratefully proclaim that I am a dedicated adherent of traditional spirituality of the Anishinaabe.

I am a born again pagan.

Notes

1   Russell, Bertrand (1957). *Why I Am Not a Christian, and other essays on religion and related subjects.* New York, NY: Simon and Schuster.

2   Einstein, Albert (1931). *Living Philosophies: A series of intimate credos.* Brooklyn, NY: AMS Press Inc.

3   Wright, Ronald (1992:1–2). *Stolen Continents: The Americas Through Indian Eyes Since 1492.* New York, NY: Houghton Mifflin Company.

4   Dickason, Olive Patricia (2002:9). *Canada's First Nations: A History of Founding Peoples from Earliest Times, Third Edition.* Don Mills, ON: Oxford University Press Canada.

5   Dickason, Olive Patricia (2002:9).

6   Indian and Northern Affairs Canada (1998:para. 2). Statement of Reconciliation: Learning from the Past. In *Gathering Strength— Canada's Aboriginal Action Plan.* Ottawa, ON: Minister of Public Works and Government Services Canada. Retrieved 31 October 2007 from: http://www.ainc-inac .gc.ca/gs/index_e.html

7   Indian and Northern Affairs Canada (1997:para. 4).

8   Assefa, Hizkias (no date:para. 17). *The Meaning of Reconciliation.* Retrieved 20 July 2007 from: http://gppac.net/documents/pbp/ part1/2_reconc.htm

9   Forced attendance was legislated in 1920 for children aged 7–15, although there are stories of children as young as age five being taken as well as accounts of forced removal before 1920.

10 In 1884, potlatches and all other cultural activities were banned, and in 1927, a prohibition was placed on creating and funding Indian political organizations.

11 Indian Residential Schools Resolution Canada (2006). *Indian Residential Schools Settlement Agreement.* Retrieved 18 September 2007 from: http:// www.irst-rqpi.gc.ca/english/pdf/ Indian_Residential_Schools_ Settlement_Agreement.PDF

12 Indian and Northern Affairs Canada (1997:para. 6).

13 Overholt, Thomas W. and J. Baird Callicot (1982:6). *Clothed-In-Fur and Other Tales: An Introduction to an Ojibwa World View.* Blue Ridge Summit, PA: University Press of America. Boston.

14 Wright, Ronald (1992:5). *Stolen Continents: The Americas Through Indian Eyes Since 1492.* New York, NY: Houghton Mifflin Company.

Biography

Fred Kelly is from the Ojibways of Onigaming and is a citizen of the Anishinaabe Nation in Treaty Number Three. He is a member of Midewewin, the Sacred Law and Medicine Society of the Anishinaabe. He is a custodian of Sacred Law and has been called upon to conduct ceremonies across Canada and in the United States, Mexico, Japan, Argentina, and Israel. He is head of Nimishomis-Nokomis Healing Group Inc., a consortium of spiritual healers and Elders that provides therapy to victims of the trauma and the horrific legacy of the residential school system. Fred is a survivor of St. Mary's Residential School in Kenora, Ontario, and St. Paul's High School in Lebret, Saskatchewan. He was a member of the Assembly of First Nations team that negotiated the historic Indian Residential Schools Settlement Agreement and continues to advise on its implementation. He has served as chief of his own community, grand chief of the Anishinaabe Nation in Treaty Number Three, and Ontario regional director of Indian and Northern Affairs Canada. Fred is fluent in the Anishinaabe and English languages and is a personal advisor to numerous First Nation leaders.

Confessions of a Born Again Pagan is written in the form of a confession. The author, now a distinguished Elder, imagines himself back in the confessional he permanently vacated at the age of fourteen. He recounts his early years in residential school and examines European ideologies and Canadian history as a way of understanding what happened to him as a boy and to his ancestors in the centuries before his birth. As a counterbalance to his early indoctrination in Catholic cosmology, he presents the Anishinaabe creation story. Fred described the thinking behind his article in the following way:

> Reconciliation processes can be personal and societal. In the personal sense, reconciliation is the means by which one regains peace with oneself. Collective reconciliation is the process that brings adversaries

to rebuild peaceful relations and a new future together. Both form the thrust of this narrative specifically on the legacy of the Indian residential schools and the conflicting interests among the policy makers, the operators, and the Survivors of that system.

Aboriginal students in front of a shrine, ca. 1960
Photographer: Sister Liliane
Library and Archives Canada, PA-213333
(This photo can also be found, along with many other resources, at www.wherearethechildren.ca)

David MacDonald

A Call to the Churches: "You shall be called the repairer of the breach" (excerpt)

On a late Sunday in August 2007, I sat in a downtown church in Halifax where the Minister read from Isaiah 58:12: "you shall be called the repairer of the breach."[1] The words spoke to authentic acts of compassion and justice. In an instant I could see what true reconciliation is all about. Years of alienation and oppression resulting from Indian residential schools require a concrete response. The challenge of reconciliation is both to know and do the truth.

Building Right Relations

In 1987, leaders of Canadian churches proclaimed a new covenant, which was issued on the fifth anniversary of the adoption of the new Canadian constitution and the *Charter of Rights and Freedoms*. It spoke specifically to the constitutional recognition and protection of Aboriginal self-government in

Canada.[2] This covenant was subsequently reaffirmed in March 2007. Behind the covenant lie many challenging and difficult years as the churches struggled to come to terms with their colonialist past. In particular, the last decade has been an agonizing one for the churches in discovering the degree to which they had participated in a ruthless program of assimilation of Aboriginal children. Stories have been told of acts of cruelty and disrespect, which are totally at odds with the stated attitude and practices of these very same faith communities. Increasingly, church members are recognizing that attitudes and acts, which were not just a part of these schools but also deeply resident in all aspects of Canadian society, run counter to what the churches themselves believe and declare.

Indian residential schools are among the most shocking and shameful realities in Canadian history. While the earliest schools predate the country of Canada itself, their full intent, impact, and reality virtually came into existence as Canada was being created. We are faced with a considerable historical dilemma. More than a hundred of these schools existed for over a century in all parts of the country, yet many people have great difficulty believing they actually existed. From the vantage point of today, one is forced to ask: *How did this happen? What was in the minds of government officials and church leaders?* There is no easy answer. While much has been written during the last several decades to describe the punishment and hardship experienced by successive generations of vulnerable children, much less has been written to explain in detail the reasoning of government and church personnel in promoting and supporting these initiatives. At the time of first contact, it would appear that the early European visitors, explorers, and traders saw the long-time resident Indigenous peoples as valuable allies in learning more about their new surroundings; certainly, they benefited from the special knowledge and skills these people possessed. There are many accounts of the friendships and intimate relations that developed. The early decades were indeed ones of exploration as well as exploitation. But by and large, they happened in the context of mutual respect and a relationship of reciprocity. The notion or the need for *reconciliation* would never have crossed anyone's mind. How far we have travelled from those earliest days.

In retrospect, it seems clear that a critical line was crossed at some point which resulted in a disastrous change in that relationship. Aboriginal people were no longer seen as equals, no longer accepted as compatriots in the adventure of knowing and benefiting from this land; instead, they were treated as wards of the state and the relationship descended into one of adversity, violence, oppression, and exploitation. Familiarity and friendship turned to fear and disrespect. As increasing numbers of European immigrants saw opportunities for a new homeland with the possibility of enormous amounts of land, their agents and officials realized they now had to solve the so-called Indian problem. This at first subtle and then increasingly profound shift in attitude and intent has proven to be one of the blackest marks on Canada's history.

Today, many people are frustrated in their attempt to make sense of Indian residential schools, land claims struggles, protests, and blockades as well as a host of Third World conditions that exist for so many First Nations, Métis, and Inuit people throughout this country. For some, the easiest explanation is to blame the victims.

We will make little progress toward resolving social, economic, educational, community, and political issues unless we understand how all this happened in the first place. Reconciliation is not even a remote possibility without some basic understanding and insight. Do we really want to know how all this happened and are we really committed to doing something about it? These are not easy questions. It is disappointing and disturbing how often we are willing to resign ourselves to what is. Without much understanding, we can come to conclusions that comfort us in our conviction that little can be done. It must also be admitted that through a combination of fear for some and special benefit for others, doing nothing sometimes seems the only answer.

I believe, however, that if reconciliation is both our goal as well as our intended course of action, then we cannot be satisfied with our state of ignorance and inactivity. We have a significant job to do. We must begin by knowing what our real history is, what it means, and what it tells us about what we must do now. Thomas R. Berger, in his book *A Long and Terrible Shadow: White Values, Native Rights in the Americas Since 1492*, suggests the attitude to Aboriginal people was finally set by the end of the War of 1812.

> There would be no wars fought to exterminate the Indians. The White population regarded the Indian culture and way

of life as primitive and anomalous. Insofar as they thought about it at all, Canadians were inclined to believe that the Indians had to be taught the arts of civilization and the duties of citizenship. As the Indians moved from what J. R. Miller calls "alliance to irrelevance," the British and their Canadian successors responded with a change of attitude from respect and gratitude to pity and contempt.[3]

This fateful shift may not have appeared ominous at the time but, in retrospect, it has been a disaster for us all. The better part of the last two hundred years has cast Aboriginal and non-Aboriginal populations into preconceived notions of who we are, what we are about, how we see one another, and therefore how we should treat one another. We know only too well the deeply entrenched stereotypes of native people in this country. They are parallel to ones that exist among Aboriginal folk. Harold Cardinal wrote the following almost forty years ago in *The Unjust Society*:

> An Indian, who probably wasn't joking at all, once said, "The biggest of all Indian problems is the white man." Who can understand the white man? What makes him tick? How does he think and why does he think the way he does? Why does he talk so much? Why does he say one thing and do the opposite? Most important of all, how do you deal with him? As Indians, we have to learn to deal with the white man. Obviously, he is here to stay. Sometimes it seems a hopeless task. The white man spends half of his time and billions of dollars in pursuit of self-understanding. How can a mere Indian expect to come up with the answer?[4]

Our modern era has set the stage to revisit our shared history of the last five hundred years. There is no doubt that some time in the twentieth century, the lowest ebb was reached in the relations between Aboriginal and non-Aboriginal people. Certainly, until the Second World War, there was an absolute and un-breachable wall between these two cultures. While it would be false to say that either side was monolithic, an overview of the situation would say this was the ultimate in two solitudes. However, beginning in the late 1940s, as the first serious questioning occurred on the wisdom of residential schools and the failure generally of any policy which dealt with native people, a dawning began to occur.

In 1964, an unlikely request from the Minister of Indian Affairs to the University of British Columbia was made "to undertake in conjunction with scholars in other universities, a study of the social, educational and economic situation of the Indians of Canada and to offer recommendations where it appeared that benefits could be gained."[5] This report, named after the chair, H.B. Hawthorn, articulated for the first time the recognition that First Nations people were "citizens plus." Alan Cairns explains Hawthorn's use of this term:

> The Hawthorn 'citizens plus' suggestion, originally directed only to the status Indian population, but capable of extension to the Inuit and the Metis, was an earlier attempt to accommodate the apartness of Aboriginal peoples from, and their togetherness with the non-Aboriginal majority. The 'plus' dimension spoke to Aboriginality; the 'citizens' addressed togetherness in a way intended to underline our moral obligations to each other.[6]

At this same time, the National Indian Brotherhood, which would eventually become the Assembly of First Nations, was founded. In 1969, the federal government's *White Paper* on Indian policy[7] ignited a storm of protest that significantly increased Aboriginal determination and solidarity. This was also the year that the churches officially withdrew from participation in Indian residential schools.

Other highlights from the last half century are undoubtedly the 1982 *Constitution Act*, particularly section 35 and the *Charter of Rights and Freedoms,* as well as the Royal Commission on Aboriginal Peoples (1991–1996) and countless subsequent decisions of the Supreme Court. Indeed, it should be said that the most consistent progress in the past quarter century has not been a result of legislative leadership but, rather, the impact of the new constitution itself and its acknowledgement through the courts. With respect to Indian residential schools, the most recent developments were the series of class action lawsuits, the Supreme Court decision (*Blackwater v. Plint, 2005*[8]) and, ultimately, the negotiations toward the *Agreement in Principle*[9] in 2005.

Now we have begun to implement the *Indian Residential Schools Settlement Agreement.* The Prime Minister has promised an apology and a truth and reconciliation commission will be created. What other actions might effectively acknowledge a new resolve to create right relations? A historic public ceremony signalling recognition and repentance, involving both civic and church leaders, would certainly be appropriate. The Governor General, Prime Minister, and other government officials, along with the primates, moderators, presidents, and archbishops of Canadian faith communities should participate. As honoured guests there should be the National Chief of the Assembly of First Nations and the leaders of all the national Aboriginal organizations. Acts of contrition and the presentation of symbolic gifts are needed. The new covenant, earlier referred to, could be expanded and endorsed by all. Concrete information and explanatory material for the media and the general public will be very important.

Overall, the churches have been given a tremendous gift and opportunity. The *Agreement* represents an opening to initiate many actions toward right relations. The next decade should be a period of working toward a new relationship that actively anticipates the next seven generations. Resonating themes might be chosen to stress our common humanity and our deep connection to the earth and to one another. We now have the opportunity to learn our true history, to repent, to apologize, to heal, to reconcile, and to restore right relations. There can be no reconciliation without right relations, and no right relationship without reconciliation. All of this sets the stage for a significant public engagement. In other words, it may become possible for the first time in several hundred years to engage in a meaningful process of truth-telling and reconciliation. But it will not be easy. There are many ways in which the process can be derailed; apathy and low expectations could lead to a situation where very little will change.

All of us will be offered the opportunity to envision and collaborate on an agenda that could begin to restore the balance and harmony that has been so badly and willfully damaged. Reconciliation is not automatic. It must be a shared journey based on mutual respect and a convivial belief in arriving at a very different and much better place. One aspect of that could be some measure of forgiveness from those who have been so seriously wounded. But, as my colleague James Scott pointed out in his presentation to the Calgary conference on Truth and Reconciliation, "Forgiveness is something that can be sought but never demanded. The request for forgiveness returns a measure of control to the wounded party. Will you forgive me?"[10]

How should we go about building a reconciliation process and agenda? Who are the ones who will be the most willing to help and participate? A First Nations person once said to me, "You should know that Aboriginal relations are fundamentally personal." I would echo that and say that the experience of reconciliation is absolutely personal. Therefore, personal contacts will be critical to building the safe and trusting relationships that can lead to reconciliation. There will need to be a preparatory stage for all parties. We will need to seriously re-examine our real history. We will be forced to question assumptions and dubious truths, which we have mostly accepted without question or concern. How can we begin to learn about one another? Can we begin the journey of walking in each other's shoes or moccasins? There will need to be some serious study and some initial steps of actually meeting one another as persons. We can hopefully work with others who have a similar experience and are also preparing for their own engagement.

We should not assume this will happen automatically. My experience is that it happens best when there is a common task and all parties have a shared investment in its success. This should not be a situation where one group is doing something for the other. There must be a real sense of partnership and mutuality. As we all work at common tasks and toward common goals, a sense of trusting and knowing the other becomes much easier. And we do share common ground. It is acutely obvious that concerns for the environment and the health of the natural world are widely and commonly shared. We should look for early opportunities to share in the joint task of healing and respecting the earth. Another more celebratory common endeavour would be participating in community activities such as sports and other games and preparing community feasts. It would be important to plan for events covering a variety of disciplines, such as sports, music, art, drama, and storytelling.

A second stage could be community building bees to build houses and community centres. Churches, temples, and mosques in towns and cities could become special places of hospitality and friendship for Aboriginal people who have relocated from traditional homelands to the less familiar urban areas. Could we not create ecumenical friendship centres where bridges of hope and purpose can be created? Parallel to these activities should be the preparation of resource materials and how-to manuals. What are the protocols and the customs that we should be aware of? There needs to be a realization that there is, in fact, significant diversity across the communities that make up the parties involved in reconciliation. We should not avoid this diversity but celebrate it.

There should also be national programs that identify leadership and rally popular support. Could there be some joint programming among the Aboriginal Peoples Television Network

(APTN), Vision TV, CPAC, and CBC Television? What about a revival of successful past programming, such as the humorous but evocative CBC Radio program Dead Dog Café? Could there also be some dynamic Internet activity that would allow young people to participate in a way that speaks to them? It will be important to have a national support system for training, resources, and networking. When there is a shared sense that all across the country people are working together in many different ways to accomplish a great task, there will be a cause for hope and great encouragement. Overall, we will need a compelling national vision of what our adventure of truth exploration and genuine and dynamic reconciliation might look like.

Our Work has Just Begun

The past twenty years or more have seen members of the Roman Catholic, Anglican, Presbyterian, and United churches struggling with the dawning reality of the historic truth of Indian residential schools. It has been a difficult and painful recognition. But in that period and preceding the *Settlement Agreement* some positive steps have been taken. All of these faith communities have struggled with and come forward with apologies as well as the establishment of initial healing funds dedicated to reaching out to those most seriously hurt. In addition, from initial defensive responses to lawsuits and allegations of criminal injury, there have been increasing attempts to resolve victim injuries through out-of-court mediation and dispute resolution. In many instances, both state and church have provided compensation. Educational materials and the designation of particular events such as the National Day of Healing and Reconciliation have also occurred.

Finally, in the process leading up to the *Agreement in Principle,* an inclusive round table process working on a full public process and a community-based approach to truth-sharing and reconciliation was developed.

The new covenant of the Christian churches signed in 1987 and reaffirmed in 2007 should be the platform for these same churches and other faith communities who choose to enter into a covenant of truth-sharing, healing, and reconciliation as the beginning of their commitment to fully live out the *Indian Residential Schools Settlement Agreement.* The historic churches who participated in Indian residential schools might hold a national service of *Apology and Repentance.* They could be part of a large, national event involving leaders of both church and state. It would announce to the Canadian public that an era of new and just purpose was being inaugurated. It would invite all citizens to actively support it.

Canada has a profound challenge and an enormous opportunity. Faith communities have an opportunity to contribute to a renewal of our respect for one another and the earth. Aboriginal peoples who have lived close to this land for millennia have a deep knowledge of the land and all its inhabitants. The wisdom of Aboriginal knowledge is one of the special gifts they may share, but the gift will only have value and meaning for Canadians at large if it is received with genuine respect for the cultures, languages and spirituality of the givers. We are being invited on a particular journey. Our destination may be less important than the experience of how we travel together.

There is particular value in examining our gifts for one another. In addition, there is a particular need to enter into acts of solidarity. Issues of justice are very much at the heart of recognizing and living out the historic treaties. Several years ago, David Arnot, Treaty Commissioner for Saskatchewan, suggested in his report that when it comes to treaties *we are all treaty people*. Most of us think that treaties refer only to status Indians, but he suggested that treaties, in fact, include all of us. How we live out those treaties is a measure of the whole quality of life of our country and all its peoples. The sooner we accept our compact with one another, the easier it will be to act in the best interests of all. Overall, ours is a task of recovering the best of what we have to offer and sharing willingly with one another. It is also the critical work of engaging in acts that build trust and the positive realization that, in our engagement, this is not a zero-sum game but an encounter with win-win possibilities. The challenge that I have set out for all of us on the road to reconciliation and forgiveness is one that people of faith should particularly understand for it is based on beliefs that we all share: at the heart of all profound spiritual truth is the call to reach out to all who have suffered unjustly and through no fault of their own. While the initial part of our response is fully acknowledging our complicity in those injustices, the greater task, I believe, will be engaging in genuine acts of healing, restoration, and reconciliation.

It is of critical importance that future generations see our generation as one that responded positively and bravely to this call to be active "repairers of the breach." We do not have all, or even many, of the answers. We will have to humbly await the lead taken by our Aboriginal sisters and brothers. Many are Survivors or descendants of Survivors who, we hope, will welcome us as companions on this journey.

Notes

1 Isaiah 58:12 RSV.

2 A New Covenant: Towards the Constitutional Recognition and Protection of Aboriginal Self-Government in Canada. A Pastoral Statement by the Leaders of the Christian Churches on Aboriginal Rights and the Canadian Constitution, originally signed February 5, 1987, reaffirmed March 9, 2007.

3 Berger, Thomas R. (1991:64). *A Long and Terrible Shadow: White Values, Native Rights in the Americas since 1492*. Vancouver, BC: Douglas & McIntyre Ltd.

4 Cardinal, Harold (1969:74). *The Unjust Society: The Tragedy of Canada's Indians*. Edmonton, AB: M.G. Hurtig Ltd., Publishers.

5 Hawthorn, H.B. (ed.) (1966:v). *A Survey of the Contemporary Indians of Canada: A Report on Economic, Political, Educational Needs and Policies in Two Volumes*. Ottawa, ON: Indian Affairs Branch.

6 Cairns, Alan C. (2001:9–10). *Citizens Plus: Aboriginal Peoples and the Canadian State*. Vancouver, BC: UBC Press.

7 Indian and Northern Affairs Canada (1969). Statement of the Government of Canada on Indian Policy, (The White Paper, 1969). Presented to the First Session of the Twenty-eighth Parliament by the Honourable Jean Chrétien, Minister of Indian Affairs and Northern Development. Retrieved 14 December 2007 from: http://www.ainc-inac.gc.ca/pr/lib/phi/histlws/cp1969a_e.html

8 Blackwater *v.* Plint, [2005] 3 S.C.R. 3, 2005 SCC. Retrieved 14 December 2007 from: http://csc.lexum.umontreal.ca/en/2005/2005scc58/2005scc58.pdf

9 Agreement in Principle, November 20, 2005. The parties to the agreement are Canada, the Assembly of First Nations, the General Synod of the Anglican Church of Canada, the Presbyterian Church of Canada, the United Church of Canada, and the Roman Catholic Entities. Retrieved 27 September 2007 from: http://www.irsr-rqpi.gc.ca/english/pdf/AIP_English.pdf

10 Scott, James V. (2007:4). The Importance of Apology in Healing and Reconciliation. Calgary T&R Conference Presentation, University of Calgary – June 14–17, 2007.

Biography

David MacDonald grew up in Prince Edward Island. He is a graduate of Prince of Wales College in Charlottetown, Prince Edward Island, and Dalhousie University and Pine Hill Divinity Hall in Halifax, Nova Scotia. David also holds several honorary degrees in law and divinity. Ordained as a United Church minister in 1961, he served as pastor in Alberton, PEI from 1962 to 1965. He is a former Member of Parliament and has served in Cabinet as Secretary of State, Minister of Communications, and Minister responsible for the Status of Women. David's commitment to social justice drew him into a variety of human rights issues within Canada as well as abroad internationally. In the 1980s he worked as logistics coordinator for the Papal Visit, Canadian Emergency Coordinator/African Famine, and later as Canada's ambassador to Ethiopia and Sudan. He led the World Council of Churches delegation to the Special Session of the United Nations on Disarmament and served as chair of the Global Network on Food Security. From 1995 to 2005, he taught at Concordia University in Quebec and, since December 1998, served as special advisor to the United Church of Canada's General Council Steering Group on Residential Schools.

Writing this paper, David remembered being introduced to Mi'kmaq culture at summer camp and, later, to Ojibway people at Lake Temagami in northern Ontario. When First Nations were granted the federal vote in 1962, he cast his ballot in the chief's house on Bear Island. While these encounters broadened his horizons, it was not until he became involved with Mi'kmaq people on Prince Edward Island that he began to truly understand how personal relationships can alter deeply entrenched attitudes that inhibit trust, respect, and goodwill among people with very different cultures and life experiences. David believes that a process of real reconciliation will require dealing directly with the major issues that have caused a rupture in the relationship between Aboriginal and non-Aboriginal peoples.

David Joanasie

Perspective on Reconciliation from an Inuk Youth

I feel I am more fortunate than others who are not as connected with their Aboriginal culture. I speak, read, and write fluently in Inuktitut and have learned and experienced Inuit culture enough to be able to practise a lot of the values and customs associated with it.

I see the connection to my (Inuit) culture as the most important aspect that has made me who I am today. In addition to that, I find it truly imperative to continue the advancement and perseverance of my mother tongue among my peers and, more importantly, among future generations.

I find it somewhat difficult to identify the role culture has within the reconciliation process. But to put it into context, and assuming that both Aboriginal (Inuit) and non-Aboriginal (*Qallunaat* or non-Inuit) cultures are included in the reconciliation process, I would say that Inuit culture is naturally susceptible to the larger Canadian culture due to its low number of carriers—by carriers I mean that there are approximately forty-five thousand Inuit in Canada within a population of over thirty-two million. This means that Inuit are a minority within a minority. *Qallunaat* culture, on the other hand, is much more assertive and plentiful when comparing it with Aboriginal cultures. It is part of the mainstream society. Also, Inuit historically are a shy people and, hence, they may be more vulnerable to large, dominant cultures.

I could see how some of these traits from either culture might hamper a sound reconciliation process. At the same time, I feel that both cultures are becoming increasingly aware of one another and are recognizing ways to work together for better understanding. The relationship between the two cultures needs to be further identified to get past historical experiences and on to a justified reconciliation process.

The role of culture within the reconciliation process, I think, is that both Aboriginal and non-Aboriginal cultures alike must respect one another in light of their historical experiences—they have to *see eye to eye* on healing, so to speak. By this, I mean that there needs to be maximized understanding and trust built between the cultures involved. It is somewhat difficult to pinpoint how this could or would be done, but it might possibly involve a whole different governing system altogether or a humungous shift in attitudes.

In reality, one of the biggest reconciliation processes that has been undertaken to date is the residential school Survivor payouts. However, money cannot buy back the experiences and fix or heal the people who have endured residential schools, including addressing intergenerational impacts and the effects on their peers, family, and community. Money is a dominant cultural concept that Inuit and other Aboriginal people have bought into and have come to value so much that it has replaced the true meaning of healing and reconciliation. What might be an option to look at further is to take a percentage of the payout to the Survivors and put it into a trust that would benefit future family, community, and nation members through the creation of materials, resources, wellness centres, counselling services, and a range of projects and services to promote, revive, and preserve language and culture. This fund could also sponsor local healing programs and invest in educational scholarships for upcoming youth and future youth in their advancement toward a better life.

These are just some of my thoughts, and I do hope they have served useful in gaining a better understanding of things and a broader perspective on reconciliation.

Biography

David Joanasie responded to our invitation to youth to write a short statement on the issue of reconciliation. David's father is Inuk and his mother is non-Inuk. David wrote:

> The reason I identify myself as being of Inuit descent is that although I am mixed blood, my entire childhood was spent

growing up in Kinngait (Cape Dorset), which is an Inuit community and, therefore, I learned to speak and live like Inuit from my community. I was born in Iqaluit, Nunavut (then Frobisher Bay, NWT) in 1983, and I currently reside in Ottawa and work for Canada's national Inuit organization, Inuit Tapiriit Kanatami (ITK).

David moved to the south to attend the Nunavut Sivuniksavut Training Program. Nunavut Sivuniksavut (NS) is a unique eight-month college program based in Ottawa. It is for Inuit youth from Nunavut who want to prepare for the educational, training, and career opportunities that are being created by the Nunavut Land Claims Agreement (NLCA) and the new Government of Nunavut. After completing NS, he accepted a job as ITK's Youth Intervenor.

David's contribution addresses the importance of cultural connections and proposes practical measures to promote healing and reconciliation in rising generations.

"Thou Shalt Not Tell Lies." Cree students attending the Anglican-run Lac la Ronge Mission School, La Ronge, Saskatchewan, 1949
Photographer: Bud Glunz, National Film Board of Canada
Library and Archives Canada, PA-134110
(This photo can also be found, along with many other resources, at www.wherearethechildren.ca)

Jose Amaujaq Kusugak

On the Side of the Angels

The Bays

The Hudson's Bay Company (HBC), or "The Bay," was incorporated on 2 May 1670,[1] making it the oldest incorporated company in the world. Two hundred and eighty years later, on 2 May 1950, I was born into the "Bay" in Naujaat (Repulse Bay), where mother and father both worked for the HBC. On my birthdays, the trader would point to the HBC insignia on their main store and give me a present, which was often a sucker candy. I would slurp it with pride to make all around me jealous with envy. The HBC, with all its own problems, was not in the Arctic to change Inuit people. It was there because of the furs it wanted to obtain from Inuit hunters, who were master hunters of Arctic animals.

Healthy hunters brought in more furs, so the HBC gave their traders minimal training on meeting the medical needs of Inuit hunters. I have even seen them pulling teeth and giving shots when necessary. Inuit and "The Bay" had a good partnership. Inuit wanted the goods and The Bay wanted the furs. The Bay boys learned Inuktitut, the language of Inuit, so there was very little assimilation of Inuit toward the *Qablunaaq* (white people) world. *Qablunaaq* HBC boys wrote several books[2] praising Inuit knowledge, culture, and perseverance. This was not from the goodness of their hearts necessarily, it was but an acknowledgement of what the HBC employees needed and wanted to learn from Inuit on Arctic survival.

Even the churches, who were appalled at the shamanistic rituals of Inuit in some regions, only wanted to save souls and not necessarily change culture. They were not necessarily anti-Inuit, but were just not Inuit. Many Inuit became Christians because the churches had what Inuit wanted: biscuits, beans, prunes, hope, and gifts of clothing from other Christians from the south. I remember there was always a strong smell of mothballs in the clothing, which is one of the first *Qablunaaq* smells we encountered.

My mother did not like the HBC's practice of stockpiling the furs of bear, fox, seal, and other fur commodities throughout the winter. But in the spring, at the first sign of break up of the creeks and rivers, she would then start cleaning the furs with sunlight soap, brisk floor brush, ulu, and flour. She would do this work until the ship came in to collect her pressed and sewn bales of fur.

An Arctic Childhood

Life as children at that time was pretty carefree. For all we knew there were at least two kinds of *Qablunaat* in this world: traders and priests. There would be an occasional airplane that came in to bring groceries and magazines. When the traders were done with the magazines, they would give them to my mother and she would then redo the wallpaper in our sod house with new pictures from the magazines with a flour-and-water paste. Sometimes, lemmings would be just on the other side of the wall-paper eating the flour. (When someone needed boils and other skin ailments tended to, my father would sometimes harvest lemmings and use them as gauzes.) A capital "H" is shaped like *aqsaaraq,* an Inuit finger-pulling game of strength. So my siblings and I would play *aqsaaraqtaaqpunga,* a game of finding capital *H*s in the magazine text on the walls. When we got tired of *aqsaaraqtaaqpunga*, we would play *nimiriaqtaaqpunga* or find-ing capital *S*s, because they were shaped like snakes or worms.

As Roman Catholics, we would go to catechism where we were taught about the "earth maker" *Nunaliuqti* (God), who was the almighty. We were taught that when His son comes down from heaven to gather believers, the ones going to heaven would go to his right side and the ones going to hell would go to his left side. It dawned on me one day that the HBC side of Naujaat would be on the left side of Jesus when he descends onto the sea, so my younger brother Cyril and I used to practise running to the church side so we would be ready when His son does come down. After one of these exercises, we came into the sod house where my mother was re-wallpapering and father was skinning foxes and smoking his corncob pipe. Mother asked why we were out of breath and, after I explained, she asked father to tell us "the truth." Father stood up slowly with his bloodied hands, messed up long hair, and, with a drag from his pipe, made a halo shape with his hair around his head. With his hands to his side dripping blood, he looked like Jesus

Christ himself, and he said, "My sons, Jesus would come down from the land side, which would put us on the right hand of God." Mother mumbled something like, "Husband!!" but that was good enough of an answer for me and my younger brother, Cyril, and off we went knowing we were safe.

We were all taught from birth our roles in life on this world. Boys were promised to girls sometimes at birth; their relationship to each other depended on their given names. Rules of life were taught, and this was communicated orally, since Inuit had no written language—history, folklore, sciences, music, rites of passage, and so on. During hardships of any kind, great care was given to having at least one survivor pass on the history. Just like the *Qablunaat*, Inuit had hypotheses and did experiments to get to the scientific conclusion. As they could not write the conclusion down, for memory they would make it into a taboo like, "If you do not follow it you will die within a year." Sometimes, messages were given in pictographs, but mostly they depicted the environment, like weather, ice conditions, fatness of caribou, husky dog behaviour, seasons, and wind directions. Anything to do with the necessities of life, we were taught to read through pictographs.

Since Inuit have an oral history and communication, lying was a "deadly sin," because it could lead to the death of someone. The number one commandment was, "Obey your father and mother and your uncles and aunts without verifiable evidence, but understand everyone or anyone else could be lying to you." The number two commandment was, "Respect the environment for you are part of it." Inuit look at themselves as part of the ecosystem. This is not to say that Inuit were a perfect race, they were not. Society control was harsh. Most people were paired off as *iviriit* or "ratters" to each other. If Inuit found you cheating, stealing, or doing unmentionables they did not approach you directly; instead, they tell your *iviq*, your "ratter." Your ratter would wait until there was a large gathering, and then put your "sins" to music and publicize your sins that way. It was a real shame to be put into a song publicly.

Inuit were socialists but kept their own implements. They could ante their things when gambling, but had to share their harvest of animals to the point that it was possible for a successful hunter *not* to get anything from his hunt, which would be a source of pride for the hunter. Until the hunter shared his harvest, his cache of meat would be stored, but it was never to be disturbed by someone else, even when found by people who were starving. This was not a law, but the people had such pride in respecting other people's "things" that they would rather starve. This did not include everyone, of course, but most people.

The whole basis of learning was through observation and through bettering what had been observed while respecting the environment. We were taught the neuroplasticity of the brain: the use of the brain is infinite. Our brain can communicate with spirits. We can transcend to check on our relatives' situation by meditating. We can become shamans by befriending spirits. This was not a religion, but a science of the brain that was achievable. The spirit world, being real of course, also had its own rules, and shamans had to follow and obey them. These are known as *tirigusungniq* or "not to hurt or break the rules of the spirits." Inuit Christians followed these rules and knew they were not breaking the commandments of the Holy Bible. Commandment number three says, "Do not serve other gods before me." It does not say do not have other gods or spirits, so long as you put Almighty God first.

Michael, my older brother, was already going to residential school in Chesterfield Inlet when I really started to remember things. There is little I do not remember after he came home after his first year. It was about the same time that my father also came home from spending time at a sanatorium in Manitoba for tuberculosis. They both had amazing stories from the South. From his experience down there, my father told us about plugging wires or ropes into walls to make lights work, of record players, and of other implements. He also spoke of tokens people had in their pockets and that they could trade these tokens at any store. Michael told us of the language he was learning in school and of the huge buildings he shared with many other Inuit of many different dialects. In this dawn of change, my younger brother and I were still just trying to figure out why the trader had brown stool and not black like the rest of us.

Ours was a strange world full of wonder. It seemed as if it could not get any better because we had everything a child could ever want. I was about seven years old and had a promised wife, whom I was very shy with, but I followed the rules and gave her everything from soap to oranges. We had many dogs, each with a name. We had freedom and rules to enjoy our freedom, and, as children, we were encouraged to be playful and have fun. We had a child's language, which we were to use until we became old enough to use a more mature Inuit language. We only heard innocent stories, as we were asked to go outside to play when the adults were discussing mature subjects. We had chores, such as getting water and training puppies. We observed as much as we were allowed to. There were rituals to keep us safe and keep us from sickness. Cyril and I were inseparable. We did everything together. We sometimes thought we were the only two people in the whole world.

Being Taken

Then one day a "flyable" took me away from our world through the sky to a dark and desolate place. I do not remember having time to say goodbye to Cyril, my soul mate. I do not remember saying goodbye to the puppies or the bright environment before we boarded the RCMP Single Otter to go to Chesterfield Inlet Residential School. I seem to remember playing with Cyril and then seeing the Union Jack put up the flagpole that signified a plane was going to come in, which was always a fun time. Perhaps, as always, the pilot would have a sucker for us, but this time the sucker was me. Michael was on the plane with me. He was my older brother but he was not Cyril. Perhaps we were close at one time, but his time in the residential school had alienated us somewhat. Still, because he was a sibling and of blood, I hung on to him. I did everything he did. When he looked out the window of the plane, I searched to see what he was looking at. When he closed his eyes, I did too, but opened mine often to see if he had opened his. I observed everything he did as I was taught to observe and do. I was on my own now, still a child with Inuit child language, not old enough to be on my own. But now, my childhood was behind me. I was on my own. I thought perhaps Judgment Day had come and we were going to a very happy place, but then again the plane landed on the sea.

I remember fish swimming under the pontoons of the plane. I remember being carried by one of the pilots to the beach, whimpering and thinking we were going to be left behind. The pilots smiled and spoke gibberish to us, and, before sunset, we took off again to finish our trip, which I had hoped would never end. The unknown was numbing to think about. Because time must elapse, it did, and too soon we landed in the dark on a lake somewhere. I do not know about the other children, but I was now following my brother and not focusing on anything else. He was all I had left. He probably talked to me, but the fear was overwhelming so I tried not to see or focus on anything else. I would then hang on to my older brother for the rest of the trip. Everyone else and everything was black.

The School

Entering "the hostel," it was impossible to ignore all your senses. Strange voices and languages could be heard in the distance, strange new smells permeated the air at the doorway, and everything was painted in white, in contrast to the people in black. My brother and I were immediately separated, as we were seemingly separated by size. Now, I was alone, alone as I had never been before. A cry was in my throat, but being there with other children my size, it was not the right thing to do. I did not cry and did as little as possible so as to not attract attention from the Sisters (nuns). We were taken to the kitchen and mess hall and then given tea and "Roman Catholic" biscuits. In Repulse Bay, Roman Catholic biscuits were rare so we always ate them slowly to see who would have the last enviable mouthful. But in my new world, "*vite!!*" was the word being repeated. One of the nuns would put her hand under the children's chins, making them chew faster and repeating this word "*vite, vite…!!*" From that moment on, *vite* became a normal word, as we were to do most things in a hurry. When we did not *vite*, we were half lifted by the ear and made to *vite*.

After tea and biscuits, I had to pee, but had no way of knowing how to ask and dared not attract more attention than necessary. I thought surely they would take us outside to pee or maybe to a real toilet room like the HBC staff house. Instead, we were led into the bedroom—the biggest room I had seen in my life up to that time—and told to undress and put on a new set of soapy-smelling clothes. The nun mumbled many meaningless things, but I kept my head down like the huskies we controlled lest we yelled at them more. I eyed where they put my brother and, after what sounded like "Hail Mary," we were put to bed. The nun went to every bed and made sure that we all had our hands visible on top of the blankets (apparently, I later learned, so that we did not masturbate) and out went the lights.

In Repulse Bay, I had shared a bed with my brother Cyril all my life, and now I was sharing with a room full of seemingly countless children who spoke, cried, walked, and tossed and turned. I tried to not move in case one of the sleepwalkers came my way, and then sometime during the night, I fell asleep looking towards my brother's way.

I remember dreaming, not of family or of home, but about this kid who we were told about during catechism. He was trying to empty the ocean with a spoon. The point, apparently, was that it was impossible. I remember always thinking it was possible. Anyhow, he put out his hand holding a thimble and told me to pee in it. I told him I should not, but he was so peaceful and innocent and he was in our catechism, so I relented and peed in the thimble, at first holding back so I did not overflow it. Then, when it did not overflow, I let out a flood. To my surprise, I relieved myself without ever filling the thimble. When he proceeded to carefully pour the thimble into the spoon, I woke up to the nun doing her wake-up call. I saw then that everyone was wearing the kind of clothing I was given the night before, and the nun was holding the same kind of clothing herself. She made folding motions, which everyone else was doing, so I folded my dripping-with-pee clothes and put them under my pillow as instructed. I followed others in the procedure of washing, brushing teeth, and breakfast and then went to my first day of school.

The first morning of school was surprisingly nice, as the creatures of the night before were a distant memory now. We were even given hot chocolate, a rare drink in Repulse Bay, and then we took a nap. This is not so bad, I thought. The morning ended too fast, it seemed, when we had to go back to the hostel for lunch. At least that was what they told us. At the hostel doorway, our supervisor was waiting and nudging everyone as they went by her in a single file. Since the morning went so well I had my head up to observe what other children were doing so I could do the same. I stepped up to the nun and waited for a nudge, but instead of a nudge, I got pulled by the ear and, nearly hanging in the air, I hopped alongside her while willing myself not to cry.

We stopped next to my bed with the sheets pulled out. She made it obvious that she wanted me to carry them, so I did. I could hardly see over the sheets, blanket, and pajamas in front of me, but I did not have to as my ear was leading me to my next stop, a washing tub. I washed the sheets and pajamas with a bar of soap and wrung them out as much as I could. The nun kept yelling gibberish to me throughout "lunchtime," and by the time I was finished, it was time to go back to school. I asked what my school friends had for lunch and was told frozen fish, biscuits, and tea. Frozen fish? In the summer? How do you freeze fish in the summer? Their answer was, "I do not know." School was fun though. We learned many things we never knew existed. All the trees had apples or oranges. There were bears of different colours. We counted numbers that went beyond twenty.

There was a *Qablunaaq* boy named Dick who had a funny-looking dog. Singing, art, and science were my favourite subjects. One day our teacher told us that plants grow because of water and that if we water plants we can help them grow. During recess I found fall flowers and watered them daily, and sure enough, they seemed to be growing. When freeze-up time came I made a little snow shelter for them and continued to water them. Then one day a blizzard came and I could not find them anymore, but I thought about them throughout the year, and the following spring I found them again. The ice buildup had protected them.

They also taught us to play bingo. At my first bingo game I won cigarettes. I was so happy they asked me to give these to some older Inuk, and, later, a teacher gave me a skunk figurine. We also played "mass" with child-size chalices, tabernacle, robes, and so on. One evening, when we were playing mass, we heard this girl crying with all her might. Then we saw it was Amia, the oldest girl in the hostel, being dragged down the stairs by her long hair. She was holding her own hair with both hands so the nun would not pull it out by the roots. She was made to apologize for saying "bad things" to some boy. I felt some guilt as she was the girl the oldest boy used to have me deliver messages to about where to meet. I was the youngest child in the school at the time and getting picked on horribly by a gang of older children. Amongst other things, they would stick a knife into the snow with the blade up and I was forced into a push-up position over the knife. They would then take turns stepping on my back. One day the oldest boy said he would protect me from anyone if I would take messages to the oldest girl, which I gladly did for the protection. He kept his word and no one bothered me after that.

Abuse

One day I heard there was "abuse" at the school. It reminded me of my mother, who had spent time at a nun convent, telling us before we left for the residential school that we should never be touched on certain parts of our body. I guess she knew "things" about certain priests or brothers. Later on, her words served well for me and, apparently, my older brother, as many of the unfortunate victims were terribly sexually abused. (I only learned of this as an adult after the residential schools issue started coming out.) These were some of the boys I went to school with, and they never shared any of this as they were kept silent with threats. One of them told me they were made to sit side-by-side naked while they were waiting to be taken to the Brother's bed to service him one by one. When one was done, he would have to tell the next boy it was his turn, and so on.

I have not heard these horrible stories about the nuns except from one boy, who I do not believe as he lied about too many things. He claims to have been sexually abused by nuns, but I think he is just ashamed to admit it was from the same Brother.

Bad Times, Good Times

For all the horrible stories, there are as many or more happy stories: Christmas plays, feasts, letters from home, bishop visits, anointings, learning new things, coming of spring, last days of school, and going home. Bishop visits were particularly happy occasions. All the rooms were transformed with colourful, silky coverings—light pink, yellow, and purple. All the beds were

covered with these magical covers. High Mass was done royally
with all the priests in their finest, with canes, hats, and fine
jewellery. The Gay Pride parade in Toronto would be jealous
of this. As fast as the magic appeared, it disappeared when the
bishop left. Everything was dark and gloomy once again.

When spring was coming, things seemed to ease, or perhaps
our minds were preoccupied with thoughts of home. There
were snowless patches of earth to play in, lemmings to kill,
puddles to jump into, and punishments that did not seem to
happen as often. The frozen fish, whale blubber (*maktaaq*),
caribou, and other meats were not so frozen at suppertime.
Cleaning up classrooms and school things meant that the time
of going home was coming soon. We just could not count the
days, as we never knew until we were *vited* to the airplane.

Going Home

Going home after being away for ten months brought thoughts
of puppies, little sister, mother and father, and of course Cyril.
But the truth is that one can never really go home again. My
family had grown more at home. Cyril had matured a year as
an Inuk. His Inuit language had changed, his observations and
doings were beyond mine as an Inuk. Yes, I had learned some
foreign knowledge, but I had not aged at home. The puppies
grew up, my sister was no longer a baby, and my parents acted
differently towards me as they were not quite sure how to address me or how I would react. My language and mannerisms
were still so childish after a year and being away. But after some

minor tweaking adjustments, Cyril and I had two months to be who we were and are: two free spirits with much to learn from each other. We laugh heartily because we now have brown stool just like the white folk.

Year of the Apology

For many years I had argued within myself over the good and the bad of going to residential schools. I always sided with the government and the churches as I thought they were on the side of angels. They were only following a curriculum that had no Inuit cultural content at all. They could only teach what they knew and, of course, they could not teach what they did not know. I knew there were exercises where students were not allowed to speak their mother tongue, but in linguistic terms, this is known as a "full immersion" language course. I had not learned about hunting, skinning, and igloo building because I had not had the opportunity. I heard this assimilation was intentional, but it could have been done so smoothly that I did not know that it happened to me. I am observant because I am Inuk and smart enough to know that, as an Inuk, I am way behind students who quit school or never went. I know less than them about Inuit culture and language, but that goes with the territory.

I was asked by Inuit Tapiriit Kanatami to join Mary Simon in attending Prime Minister Harper's "offer of full apology on behalf of Canadians for the Indian Residential Schools system."[5] Unfortunately, I was committed to going somewhere else, but on 11 June 2008, I listened to every word on the CBC Radio:

"the federal government, partly in order to meet its obligation to educate aboriginal children, began to play a role."[6] That was why my mother blindly allowed us to be taken away year after year. The Prime Minister continued:

> Two primary objectives of the residential system were to re-move and isolate children from the influence of their homes, families, traditions and cultures, and to assimilate them into the dominant culture. These objectives were based on the assumption aboriginal cultures and spiritual beliefs were in-ferior and unequal. Indeed, some sought, as it was infamously said, 'to kill the Indian in the child.'[7]

For some reason I missed my mother then. I was numb and had an uncontrollable urge to cry, but the residential school had taught me to keep my cry underground. I cry when I am alone. After *mamiattugut* (the apology) and "forging a new relation-ship between aboriginal peoples and other Canadians,"[8] I made a hard copy of the text and went to board my plane to deal with the Dene/Inuit Manitoba border issue.

Thank you all who made this happen. You have achieved no less than Mahatma Gandhi and Martin Luther King, Jr. achieved for their people. They have freed us through peace and persis-tence and that includes you, Prime Minister.

Merci, thank you, *masi cho, qujannamiik!*

Remember, though, we are all accountable for things we do and for things we do not do.

Notes

1   More information on the history of the Hudson's Bay Company can be found at: http://www.hbc.com/hbcheritage/history/

2   Samples of these books can be found online at The Champlain Society Digital Collection website: http://link.library.utoronto.ca/champlain/search.cfm?lang=eng (There are 26 documents with digitized sample pages if one searches for key words "Inuit or Eskimo.")

3   See: Clark, Michael and Peter Riben (1999). *Tuberculosis in First Nations Communities, 1999.* Ottawa, ON: Minister of Public Works and Government Services Canada (retrieved 1 April 2009 from: http://www.hc-sc.gc.ca/fniah-spnia/alt_formats/fnihb-dgspni/pdf/pubs/tuberculos/1999_commun-eng.pdf); and CBC (2007). Nunavut health group to commemorate Inuit TB victims, CBC News, Tuesday, September 11, 2007. Retrieved 1 April 2009 from: http://www.cbc.ca/canada/north/story/2007/09/11/nu-tb.html

4   King, David (2006:1). *A Brief Report of the Federal Government of Canada's Residential School System for Inuit.* Ottawa, ON: Aboriginal Healing Foundation.

5   Prime Minister Harper offers full apology on behalf of Canadians for the Indian Residential Schools system. June 11, 2008. Ottawa, ON: Office of the Prime Minister. Retrieved 4 September 2008 from: http://www.pm.gc.ca/eng/media.asp?id=2149

6   Prime Minister Harper's statement of apology.

7   Prime Minister Harper's statement of apology.

8   Prime Minister Harper's statement of apology.

Biography

Jose Amaujaq Kusugak was born in 1950, in an igloo in Naujaat (then Repulse Bay), located on the Arctic Circle. He is the second oldest of 12 children. Both of his parents had worked for the Hudson's Bay Company; his father was a handyman and his mother worked as a cleaner and fur washer. Jose went to school in Chesterfield Inlet, Nunavut, and Churchill, Manitoba. He attended high school in

Saskatoon, Saskatchewan. After graduation, he returned to Rankin Inlet, Nunavut, to work at the Eskimo Language School, a branch of the University of Saskatchewan. Later, he taught Inuktitut and Inuit history at Churchill Vocational Centre.

Jose has been active in Inuit politics since 1971, shortly after the founding of the Inuit Tapiriit Kanatami (ITK) (then Inuit Tapirisat of Canada). He persuaded the new organization of the critical need to standardize the written Inuit language, which is primarily an oral language. However, funding for this project had been delayed, so Jose worked as an assistant to Tagak Curley, the first president of ITK, and introduced the concept of land claims to Inuit in the Arctic. In 1974, he went to Alaska to study how the land claims process worked there. From 1980 to 1990, Jose worked as the area manager of CBC in the Kivalliq (Keewatin) region. He served as president of Nunavut Tunngavik Incorporated, one of four regional organizations that make up ITK, from 1994 to 2000. He was elected president of ITK in June 2000. He describes the relationship of the Inuit to Canada as First Canadians, Canadians First. Jose and his wife, Nellie, live in Rankin Inlet, Nunavut, and they have four grown children.

[The editors acknowledge the passing of Jose Kusugak at the age of 60 on 19 January 2011 in his home town of Rankin Inlet.]

Inuit board the C.D. Howe for medical and eye check-ups
Kimmirut (formerly Lake Harbour), Nunavut, 1951
Photographer: Wilfred Doucette
Library and Archives Canada, PA-189646
(Courtesy of Legacy of Hope Foundation's "*We were so far away...*": *The Inuit Experience of Residential Schools* exhibit)

Rita Flamand

Truth about Residential Schools and Reconciling this History: A Michif View

Oppression by the Government of Canada and the Catholic Church has had a major negative influence on the Métis people. The natural evolution of a culture, a nation of people, and a society in all its aspects was thwarted by the government-sanctioned influence of the Church. Inadequate education, loss of language, and loss of culture were the results. *Culture* is defined as "the integrated pattern of human knowledge, belief, and behavior that depends upon the capacity for learning and transmitting knowledge to succeeding generations ... the customary beliefs, social forms, and material traits of a racial, religious, or social group."[1]

The effects of colonization and its mission are intergenerational and have resulted in the many social problems affecting today's generation. In addition, many Métis people suffered mental, physical, and emotional abuse caused by the inter-generational effects of residential school, and it still continues today through the loss of language and culture. In order for our children to know where they are going, they must know where they came from so that they can move forward in a healthy way. There is also a need for adequate and accessible healing programs and therapies that should be made available to Métis people.

My good friend and pupil, Darlene Kemash, sat down with me recently to assist in the telling of my story. You see, I speak and write in Michif, and Darlene helped to translate and organize my words.

This is my story ...

Ni Maamaa Ste-Anne de Lima Fagnan

My mother, the storyteller of our family, related this story to us about the residential school she attended when she was a little girl:

> *Kétatawé iko ni'kushopayhin* (all of a sudden I came to), I was standing on top one of the corner beds in our dormitory. *Trwaa kémaa kaatr lii seur ota aanavañ kaa niipawichihk* (there were three or four nuns there standing around in front of me). As I tried to take in what happened, I focused my eyes on Sister Frances who was standing directly in front of me. The headpiece of her habit was dangling on her shoulder all askew. Forgetting everything, my eyes popped open! SHE HAD HAIR!! Us girls used to wonder if the nuns had hair,

and we sometimes wondered if they had feet the way they used to glide around in their long skirts. I was horrified when I learned that I had grabbed Sister Frances' headpiece off her head! As I looked around, the beds were all messed. I was apparently jumping from bed to bed as they tried to catch me.

Having some kind of breakdown, my mother had started fighting with the Sisters. My mother was Métis, and the reason she was in the residential school was to fill the quota while they were in the process of rounding up Treaty Indian children from the north to fill the school. In the meantime, Métis children would do. After six or seven years in the residential school, my mother could barely write her name. It always bothered her that she could not read or write. My dad would just hold that over her. After all, he went up to grade 4. She would ask him to teach her to read and write and, inevitably, their sessions would end in a fight with my mom accusing my dad of teasing and laughing at her. She wanted her children to have the education she never had. Little did she know that her children and grandchildren, second and third generation, would suffer some of the same fate with the priest and nuns, although we went to a Catholic day school.

My Parents

My mother, Ste-Anne de Lima Fagnan, was known by the name of Anne, although a lot of people still called her Ste-Anne, and she was called *"mii mii"* by her grandchildren. She did not want to be called Ste-Anne. She used to say that she was not a saint. She was born in Camperville, Manitoba, on

7 October 1905. Her parents lived on a little farm a couple of miles outside of Camperville. They used to come to town once in a while to get some supplies. My father, Peter Flamand, was born on 27 March 1886 in St. John's, North Dakota, a year after the Riel Resistance. It was not safe for my grandmother to have her baby in Canada, as the Métis people were always on the run from the RCMP. This was a very sad time for the Métis. But my dad's parents, my grandparents, still managed to run a farm in the Inglis, Manitoba area.

In the early nineteen hundreds, my grandparents, Joseph Flamand and Agathe Fleury, along with a lot of Métis people from the south, came to the Camperville area, drawn by the good fishing in Lake Winnipegosis. My Uncle Cyril was the first son to get here, as my mother recollects. She said the girls were talking about him as the "new guy in town." Not long after, she said the girls were saying "another one of Joe Flamand's sons got here and he's better-looking." My Mother said, "I saw him and I didn't think he was good-looking." With my mom this meant that she thought he *was* good-looking. She said she only saw him a few times, until one Sunday one of her sisters was shaking her awake early in the morning, *"wanishkaa, wanishkaa ki wii wiikitoon"* (get up, get up, you are getting married). She asked her sister, "What are you talking about?" Her sister told her, "Last night, Pete Flamand came to see Papa while you were sleeping and we heard them talking. He asked Papa for your hand in marriage and Papa said 'yes.'"

Where We Were Born

My older brothers were born in Saskatchewan because my parents, after they were married, went where the jobs were. My mom used to tell us that two or three families would travel together by horse and wagon across the Prairies. They would meet different Métis and Indian families also travelling by wagon and would set up their tents and visit together for a few days while they rested their horses. Later on, my parents settled back in Camperville where the rest of us were born. There were five girls and five boys in my family. I often wonder how my dad fed us all. I only remember everything tasting so good, but maybe it was because I was always hungry.

Of course we lived off the land. We ate nothing but wild meat and fish, and my dad always had a big garden. We picked berries in the summer. There were so many berries in those days, and we lived in the blueberry patch for part of every summer. I was quite young, and all we did as kids was play! It was so nice and sandy where we pitched our tents; this place was called *kaa napaksakokaatek* (where it is flat). The tents were pitched all around and we, the kids, would play in the middle where it was safe. We always played outside, not like the kids today, playing video games and becoming dangerously overweight. When I was a kid, there were no overweight kids around.

My mom would take us all to pick blueberries, and we, being the younger ones, would have a nap in the bush. My mom used to put cotton batting in our ears so the bugs would not crawl in. When we would get back to camp later, we would see fires starting outside the tents and women making supper. What I remember is my mom cooking fried blueberries in lard with sugar right away because it was quick to prepare and it would turn into a blueberry *rubaboo*. We would eat that with *la galet* to tide us over until the meat and veggies were cooked. Those are such good memories.

School

We lived about a mile from the school. It was hard trudging to school through the high snow in the wintertime and in water in the spring. I was six when I started school. I could not speak English. I only spoke Michif. The schoolroom was overflowing with kids—there were kids standing all around the room. Our teacher was a young Ukrainian man. All I remember was us kids standing around him while he was doing a strange dance called the *Kolomeika*. His long legs were flying off the floor. We were used to jigging, but this was a new twist.

English, Saulteaux, and Michif were being spoken in the classroom. It was confusing. When the teacher said to someone, "Go to the cloakroom," they would come out crying. I learned that they got the strap when they went in there. One day he looked straight at me and said, "Go to the cloakroom." I was terrified and hung my head and started to cry. He must have forgotten about me in the chaos when he saw me crying, as he told my sister to ask me if I was sick. I understood the word "sick," so when she asked me, I said "yes." He sent me home and my mother kept me home for the rest of that year.

Day School

When I went back the following year, there was a change in our school. It was now called Christ the King School, and the nuns from the residential school were in charge. We were not allowed to speak our language. Everything was in English. I was learning two languages in school, English in the classroom and Saulteaux out in the schoolyard. A quarter of us kids spoke Michif and the rest spoke Saulteaux. I understood some Saulteaux words because my mom and my *kohkum* used to speak Saulteaux when they did not want us to understand something. English was totally alien, but coming from a day school, we did not lose our language completely because we spoke it at home in the evenings.

The nuns would arrive by horse and buggy every morning with their supplies and lunch for the day. They would start warming up their food at around 11:30 A.M. They would fry potatoes in butter. Oh, how that used to smell so good! By the time we went home for our lunch or ate it in the corner at school, it was hard to swallow bannock and lard or the morning's cold porridge with that smell lingering in your nose. The priests were always there having lunch with the nuns. After lunch, a priest would play with us and take us girls to the mission on the pretense of helping him in the Shomoo Hall. There, he would grab and touch us inappropriately. I did not feel right, but he was like God after all. That is how holy we thought they were.

Our family, parents, and grandparents were always in church. My grandma used to dress like a nun in long black dresses with a big cross around her neck. We would never tell them when the priests would rub us against them, especially Father "B..." I can still hear his high-pitched, excited laughter when he would be around us. We were so innocent we thought they loved us, and that is how they got away with it. They knew we would not say anything. We were about eight to ten years old. They controlled us right from when we started going to confession—that dark confessional in the back we seemed to be always attending—which was a form of control and abuse. We had to confess everything, our bad thoughts as well as all our sins. Did we have bad thoughts about a boy? What were they? If we kissed him it was a mortal sin, at least twenty Hail Marys.

Although we went to day school, the priests controlled all the Métis people in many different ways. I remember when the second-hand clothing would arrive. The women would come to get clothes for their kids and themselves. The priest would get the women to try on the tops and blouses, touching them on the breasts and saying, "Oh, it's too big" or "too small," while running his hands down the breasts pretending to straighten the blouse. The women would laugh embarrassingly. My girlfriend used to have big breasts, and we used to think the nuns were jealous because they were always making mention of her "big *tootoosh*" in a derogatory way. She used to make me tie a folded *koosh* (diaper) around her chest. I would pin it in the back with safety pins so she would have a flat chest.

Pagan Babies

We used to have a big drawing of a pyramid on the wall of our classroom. Our names were written on a coloured star at the bottom. Every time we brought a penny to school, our star would move up a notch. We worked our way up that pyramid with every cent we could muster up (there were not as many pennies to be had in them days). By the time we got to the top, it was five dollars and, *voila*!! We had bought a pagan baby! I used to wonder where these pagan babies were. I always thought they were some poor babies somewhere across the ocean. Imagine my surprise when I later learned the pagans were my Indian cousins and relatives.

Praying in School

We used to pray a lot in school. We would kneel down and pray when we arrived in the morning, when we went for recess, before lunch, after lunch, and again before we went home. I kid you not, my knees used to be red, flat, and sore. One day, when the nun was going to strap my sister (we had a big, black leather strap that was used in class), I got so angry that I told the nun, "We don't learn anything in here anyway, all we do is pray." I went home but my dad brought me back. The nun made me stand in front of the class and apologize for being mad at her.

Residential School

The church and residential school were two or three miles from my home, and we used to walk to the "mission," as we called it. That is where the church, residential school, Fathers' and Sisters' residences, and barns were clustered. It used to be so cold to walk to church, especially when you would hit the field close to the church. The wind used to be so cold off the lake, but we were promised we would go straight through to heaven if we went to Holy Communion for nine consecutive first Fridays of each month. We would be there for early Mass, and we would make several of those first Fridays. So you see, I will be going straight to heaven when I die.

On Sundays, we would go to church in the big church. Each Sunday, we would watch these two doors open on each side of the altar, and the little girls would come out of one door and the boys out of the other. The girls would be all dressed in cotton dresses, all the same kind. Their hair was cut straight across the forehead and below the ears. I used to envy their nice dresses and shoes as I did not have nice dresses like that. The boys came out of the other door, all dressed in black suits and neckties and with short hair. They too had to march to the back of the church and up to the balcony where there was a big pipe organ. They had the sweetest voices you ever wanted to hear. I remember on Christmas Eve they used to sing *Christ the Messiah*. They were every bit as good as any choir. The choir sang in Latin, and the altar boys served the priests during Mass, answering the priests in Latin.

I do not remember seeing them smile. They always looked serious. I did not know where they came from. They just seemed to always be there. I would hear *"aasha mina kii tapaashiiwak aatit"* (some of them ran away again) and *"Maaka kii mishkawewak*" (but they caught them). Then, during Sunday Mass, they would be lined up in front of the church where the entire congregation would see them. Sometimes they would be a mixture of boys and girls, but most times they would either be all girls or all boys. Their heads would all be shaven. They would stand there with their heads down, very embarrassed. I used to wonder where they were from. I never heard anyone talk about them around the village, just in whispers, as if the people were scared the priests and nuns would hear them.

When my cousins from Tanner's Reserve[2] started attending the mission school, I became more aware that the kids who appeared in church actually lived at the mission. After that, we would go with my grandparents every Sunday after Mass. We were allowed to see them in the waiting room for just one hour. Even those kids that were from the reserve were only allowed to see their parents for one hour. Sometimes, the nuns would take the "mission kids," as we used to call them, for a walk on the highway. There would be nuns in front of them, on each side of them, and behind them, walking them like prisoners. We could not even wave at our cousins. We would run in the ditch, trying to get their attention, but the nuns would chase us away.

The Catholic Church has so many rituals, and we seemed to be always going to church. We went for catechism, Benediction, and Lent and, during the month of May, honoured the Virgin Mary. The priests were always behind the holy altar. To us they seemed so mysterious and holy, almost Christ-like. That is how the people saw them. Our parents did not teach us the Bible or catechism, the nuns and priests did. I completed grade 8. For

us, education ended at grade 8 as there was no further class for
Métis children. Our school only went up to grade 8, there was
no high school. After that we had to get out and find a job. We
were cheated out of a high school education.

Truth and Reconciliation

The Canadian government must acknowledge the cultural
genocide and abuse of the Métis people at the hands of the
government and the Catholic Church. A public acknowledgement and apology by the Government of Canada and the
Catholic Church is the first step towards reconciliation. With
acknowledgement, the true history of Métis people must be
made available in the school curriculum, not only for our
Métis children, but for all Canadian children. Research,
curriculum development, and implementation must happen.
Human and financial resources must be allocated. Elders must
be interviewed and their history documented. We were an
integral part of the forming of this nation, and we remain so.

Also, the Michif language must be taught in schools where
Métis children attend. Culture is conveyed through language.
The government must recognize the importance of the Michif
language as an integral part of health and wellness for Métis
people. This should include curriculum development and implementation, with human and financial resources allocated for
this. Also, Michif Elders and speakers must be consulted while
they are still living. As my story shows, along with many other
Métis people's stories, there were many Métis who were also

victimized by residential schools (including day schools), so we too should be a part of the truth and reconciliation process.

Notes

1   *Merriam-Webster's Collegiate Dictionary*, Tenth Edition, s.v. "culture."

2   Also called Gambler's Reserve at Silver Creek in Manitoba. During my childhood, the people living there were almost all from the Tanner family and were all Michif speakers. See Barkwell, Lawrence J. with Dr. Peter Lorenz Neufeld (2007). *The Famous Tanner Family and Tanner's Crossing, now Minnedosa, Manitoba.* Winnipeg, MB: Louis Riel Institute. Retrieved 5 February 2009 from: http://www.metismuseum.ca/resource.php/07238

Biography

Liza Rita Flamand is a Métis Elder born 28 August 1931 in the community of Camperville, Manitoba. She attended Christ the King School, a day school taught by nuns and priests of Pine Creek Residential School and the Roman Catholic Church. Rita and her husband raised eight children, and she is known as Kohkum to her sixteen grandchildren and six great-grandchildren. Rita completed an LPN course at St. Boniface, Manitoba, in 1948 and later nursed in several hospitals throughout Manitoba, Ontario, and British Columbia.

Rita is currently President of Mine'igo Sipi Senior Inc. and of Camperville Métis Cemetery. She was President of Home & School and Councillor on the Community Council. She also coordinated and facilitated programs such as Community-Based University Entrance, Literacy, and Métis Education School Services programs and was employed with Community Education Development Association. Rita is a member of the Dauphin Legal Aid Advisory and Restitution committees, was certified as a Justice of the Peace Officer and Commissioner for Oaths, and worked as a Court Communicator. Rita was the first elected President of Manitoba Métis Women's Association and is a board member of both the Native Association of Community Councils and the Manitoba Métis Federation. She later became the first Coordinator of the Métis Child and Family Support program of the Manitoba Métis Federation. It was in this capacity that Rita was the first to be able to repatriate a Sixties Scoop Métis child back to her home community. Rita is endeavouring to preserve the Michif language she feels may disappear if there is no one who will take on this daunting task. Rita has put all her efforts into this since the 1980s and has since developed a Michif writing system with the assistance from two linguists: Peter Bakker, University of Aarhus, Denmark, and Robert Papen, Université du Québec à Montréal, Québec. In 2000, she began teaching and tutoring both adults and children the Michif language from lessons she developed herself.

Since 1999, Rita has translated into Michif numerous books, guides, and newsletters on Métis language, history, recipes, and stories for both adults and children. In 2006, she contributed to the book *In the Words of Our Ancestors: Métis Health and Healing*. Rita continues to translate and teach the Michif language.

Métis family at Fort Chipewyan, Alberta, 1899
Photographer unknown
Glenbow Archives, NA-949-118
[Reprinted from the Legacy of Hope Foundation's *Where Are the Children?* exhibit catalogue (2003)]

Fred Hiltz

Remembering the Children: The Church and Aboriginal Leaders Tour

[The following are the remarks made by the Most Reverend Fred Hiltz, Primate of the Anglican Church of Canada, in Ottawa, Ontario on 2 March 2008 during the Church and Aboriginal Leaders Tour.]

Today marks the beginning of an Aboriginal and Church Leaders Tour with stops in Ottawa, Vancouver, Saskatoon, and Winnipeg to promote awareness and anticipation of the Truth and Reconciliation Commission to be established by the federal government in consultation with the Assembly of First Nations.

In a recently published volume, *From Truth to Reconciliation: Transforming the Legacy of Residential Schools* (produced by the Aboriginal Healing Foundation Research Series), we read in the introduction:

> Aggressive civilization to accomplish colonial goals was thought to be futile in the case of adults. Residential school-ing was the policy of choice to reshape the identity and

consciousness of First Nations, Inuit, and Métis children. The persistence of colonial notions of superiority is evidenced in the fact that residential schooling ... punished the expression of Aboriginal languages, spirituality, and life ways and attempted to instill a Euro-Canadian identity in Aboriginal children.[1]

This policy of assimilation had its origin in *The Gradual Civilization Act* of 1857. It was reinforced by *The Indian Act* of 1876 and sanctioned by successive Canadian Parliaments. The language used to describe this policy was itself disturbing, for it spoke of removing children from their "evil" surroundings. Simply stated, the "savage" child would be remade into a "civilized" adult.

The Church had a significant role in this program of assimilation in that we provided the teaching staff and supervised a number of the residential schools. The Anglican Church of Canada, which I represent, ran 24 of these schools concurrently through the 1920s. Over time, we ran 36.[2]

The theme of the walk we begin today is "Remembering the Children." They were taken far from home and family and then denied their language and culture as we went about remaking them in our image. The children were punished for speaking their language. They were abused physically, emotionally, and sexually. Many were scarred for life. Many survived their experiences. Many others went missing. Many died.

As churches we have *so much* for which to be *so sorry*. In August 1993, Archbishop Michael Peers offered an apology to

Aboriginal peoples on behalf of the Anglican Church of Canada at the National Native Convocation in Minaki, Ontario. His apology included the following statement:

> I know how often you have heard words which have been empty because they have not been accompanied by actions. I pledge to you my best efforts, and the efforts of our church at the national level, to walk with you along the path of God's healing.[3]

Fifteen years later, the Anglican Church of Canada, along with other churches, views the establishing of the Truth and Reconciliation Commission as a very significant step along the long road toward the healing of which Archbishop Peers spoke.

The Truth and Reconciliation Commission will provide an opportunity for survivors of the residential schools to tell their stories. It will enable those who listen to grieve with them as they speak of how they were robbed of their language and culture, how their dignity was diminished, how their bodies were abused, and how their spirits were broken. It will enable Canadians to begin coming to terms with the long-term impact of the residential schools. It will enable Canada to compile an honest, accurate, public, and permanent record of the residential schools. At a January 2008 gathering of Anglicans involved with work arising from the legacy of abuse in residential schools, Esther Wesley (co-ordinator for the Anglican Indigenous Healing Fund) spoke of the need for a Truth and Reconciliation Commission clearly and directly. She said, "This is a history that belongs to all of us. It belongs to all Canadians and we need to know our history to prevent it from ever happening again."

When the truth has been told and the truth received, when the truth has been borne and properly recorded, then we shall be much further along the path of understanding that will lead to reconciliation and a renewed national resolve to respect the dignity of every human being.

As church leaders, we welcome the news of the establishing of the Truth and Reconciliation Commission, and we eagerly anticipate the appointment of the commissioners. We are committed to the truth-telling the Commission calls for, and we pledge our best efforts to continue raising the profile of the Commission's work over the next five years. We recognize that the road to healing and reconciliation is a long one, and we remain committed, hand in hand, to see this journey through.

In this sacred work of "Remembering the Children," we ask for the Creator's blessing and guidance.

Notes

1 Castellano, Marlene Brant, Linda Archibald, and Mike Degagné (2008:1–2). Introduction. In *From Truth to Reconciliation: Transforming the Legacy of Residential Schools*. Ottawa, ON: Aboriginal Healing Foundation: 1–8.

2 Between 1820 and 1969, the Anglican Church ran a total of 36 schools, with its peak involvement occurring in the late 1920s, during which the Church had concurrently operated 24 schools.

3 Peers, Michael (1993). *A message from the Primate, Archbishop Michael Peers, to the National Native Convocation Minaki, Ontario*, Friday, August 6, 1993 (*see* Appendix 3). Retrieved 26 November 2008 from: http://www2.anglican.ca/rs/apology/apology.htm

Biography

Fredrick James Hiltz is the thirteenth Primate of the Anglican Church of Canada. Born in Dartmouth, Nova Scotia, in 1953, Fred has lived most of his life by the Atlantic Ocean. Fred grew up in an Anglican family in Dartmouth and was baptized at the age of four. Fred holds a Bachelor of Science degree from Dalhousie University, in biology, and a Master of Divinity at the Atlantic School of Theology. After being ordained in 1978, Fred ministered in small communities in Nova Scotia, including Sydney, Melford-Guysborough and Timberlea-Lakeside. This is where he cultivated his love for parish ministry, specifically for supporting people in times of difficulty and celebration. In 1984, Fred became the assistant priest at the Cathedral Church of All Saints in Halifax and, in 1987, became the director of the Anglican Formation Program at the Atlantic School of Theology. In 1988, he was appointed Rector of the historic St. John's Anglican Church in Lunenburg. In 1995, he was elected Suffragan Bishop of the diocese of Nova Scotia and Prince Edward Island and, later, in 2002, elected Diocesan Bishop. In July 2007, Fred was elected to the office of Primate. As chief pastor of the Anglican Church of Canada, Fred enjoys spending time with parishes and dioceses across Canada and supporting ministry on the ground. He is also committed to supporting the work of other bishops. Fred is also passionate about cultivating Anglican-Lutheran relations, both in Canada and internationally. Since 2006, Fred has co-chaired the Anglican-Lutheran International Commission. Now, as Primate, he actively works with the Evangelical Lutheran Church in Canada, a full communion partner of the Anglican Church of Canada. In January 2008, Fred took on an active role in the Primate's World Relief and Development Fund (PWRDF) when he became the first Primate to be elected president of its board. Fred is committed to promoting this Anglican social justice and development organization, which he believes is a witness to Christ's compassion. He is a strong advocate for mission initiatives in the service of the Gospel within the Anglican Church of Canada and our worldwide Communion.

Drew Hayden Taylor

Cry Me a River, White Boy

Aabwehyehnmigziwin is the Anishnawbe word for apology.
That is what Prime Minister Stephen Harper delivered in
the House of Commons on the eleventh of June 2008 to the
Survivors of Canada's residential school system.[1] Quoting the
immortal words of singer Brenda Lee, who put it so eloquently,

> I'm sorry, so sorry ...
>
> Please accept my apology ...
>
> You tell me mistakes
>
> Are part of being young
>
> But that don't right
>
> The wrong that's been done

Harper said, "We are Sorry." Sorry. Surprising words from a
surprising source. Brenda had put it much more eloquently. But
the First Nations people of Canada listened. There were thousands of Aboriginal people on the front lawn of the Parliament
buildings, eager to hear this historic admission of responsibility.
Televisions were set up in community centres, band offices, halls,

and schools in Aboriginal communities all across the country. And then the people cried. They cried at the memory of what had been done, and what was being said. This event made a lot of people cry, and for many, it was a good cry—a cathartic one. Psychiatrists and Elders will tell you that.

Since the late 1800s, over 150,000 Aboriginal children were forcibly taken away from their families and shipped off to one of 130-plus schools scattered across seven provinces and two territories. There, they were robbed of their language, their beliefs, their self-respect, their culture, and, in some cases, their very existence in a vain attempt to make them more Canadian. The key phrase I kept hearing during the apology and in the opposition responses was the misguided belief that *in order to save the child, you must destroy the Indian.* How on earth did those two thoughts become entwined? Another fine example of an un-researched and unintelligent government policy like the Chinese head tax[2] or sending a small Inuit community five hundred kilometres further north in an attempt to establish Arctic sovereignty. The thought processes of many a politician can truly be baffling when it comes to people of another race.

The official *Aabwehyehnmigziwin* was a long time in coming, and hopefully it will close the chapter on this unfortunate part of First Nations history so that an entirely new book can begin, hopefully, this time with Aboriginal people as co-authors. All of the churches who ran residential schools— Roman Catholic, United, Anglican, and Presbyterian—have issued their own version of *aabwehyehnmigziwin* over the years. In 1998, the Liberals offered a kind of watered down, wimpy, anemic version. Essentially, it was something about having "profound regrets."[3] I have a lot of regrets too. Most people do. For instance, I have had sincere regrets about some of my past relationships, but that does not mean I apologize for them. Big difference.

Perhaps it is my working-class origins and artsy nature, but I do find it odd that it was the Conservative government who found the balls to issue the *aabwehyehnmigziwin*. It makes one wonder why the Conservative lawyers saw this as possible, when ten years earlier, an army of government lawyers under the Liberals likely advised against it. You would think the residential school system would be something the Conservatives would admire. On the surface, it fits into their political and economic agenda. The government promised, in a number of treaties, to educate the youth from over 600 reserves across the world's second biggest country. They managed to download the cost of educating these youth by transferring it to the four main religious groups and their churches. Sounds like a sound economic decision, does it not?

In 2005, the Liberal government was all set to adopt the Kelowna Accord and address many of the serious issues plaguing First Nations communities. Then prime minister Paul Martin had long been concerned with Aboriginal issues. Yet no apology. Fast forward to 2006 when the Conservatives took power and offered Canada a new way of doing business, which basically involved shelving the Kelowna Accord and hiring Tom

Flanagan, author of the controversial book *First Nations? Second Thoughts*, as a top Conservative advisor. Things did not look good for First Nations communities in this new century. Then came Harper's 180-degree turn. One could almost hear the snow falling in hell. Perhaps the official bean counters had taken into account the fact that an official apology would be in their best interest, as it would shift responsibility to the Aboriginal communities. The government could then wash a lot of it off their hands.

How could the federal government know the whole issue of accountability for residential schools would later be classified as—and I love this term frequently used to describe screwed-up governmental policies—a boondoggle? It has literally come back to bite them in their fish-belly white asses. On average, over 1.9 billion dollars[4] has already been paid out to many of the approximately 80,000 Survivors of Manifest Destiny High. That is a hell of an expensive education. And the price tag is still rising. Canadian taxpayers will be buying bandages for the physical and psychological wounds their ancestors inflicted for generations.[5]

It had been obvious for a long time that apologizing was not high on the Liberals' to-do list. Pierre Trudeau did not want to bother with an *aabwehyehnmigziwin*. I think he felt it would just open the floodgates to more apologies that would quickly become unfortunate road bumps on the highway of proud Canadian history. I think he would have been right. Jean Chrétien did not believe current social beliefs should be applied to past issues, yet it was Brian Mulroney's Conservatives who issued an apology to Japanese Canadians for the country's

misdoings during World War II.[6] And now, Harper is regretting
the Aboriginal people's historical treatment. Who would have
thunk it? In all fairness, it should be mentioned that it was
the Conservatives that gave Aboriginal people the right to vote
in 1960. Way to go, Progressive Conservatives!... a phrase
I thought I would never say. Though many would argue old-
school Conservatives are substantially different from the New
World Conservatives. Personally, I think Diefenbaker could whip
Harper's ass. Still, Harper is the current boss, and I guess that
is why the Ojibways call him the *Kichi Toodooshaabowimiijim*,
which translates to "the Big Cheese" or, perhaps even more literally, to "Much Sour Milk."

Of course, there is always one spoilsport at every party, a
pisser in the pool, known as the Conservative *brain trust,* a.k.a.
Pierre Poilievre and his amazingly insensitive comments about
Survivors just needing a stronger work ethic and his opinion
that giving these people reparation money was a waste of time.
Otherwise, things might have been just fine and dandy. Evidently,
Harper took the boy out to the proverbial woodshed, and a new
and different apology by a contrite Poilievre soon followed. It
should have been expected, just like there is one drunk at every
party, one ex-girlfriend at every powwow, and one veggie burger
at every barbecue. It was bound to happen in the volatile world
of Canadian politics, somebody was going to pee in the pool.
Conservative politicians are seldom known for their subtlety.

Was the *aabwehyehnmigziwin* sincere and do I buy it? Yes, I
suppose it was sincere enough for me to buy it, however naïve

that may sound. I suppose something is better than nothing. I also know that, by very definition, politicians should not be trusted nor believed any more than a Jerry Springer guest, especially when it comes to commitments to Aboriginal people. But Harper looked sincere, as did Dion, Duceppe, and Layton—all privileged white men apologizing for the actions of other privileged white men and also eager to curry First Nation favour. It is amazing how a good education can make you the empathetic leader of a federal party and a bad education can get you an *aabwehyehnmigziwin*. They probably listened to Brenda Lee and her apologetic song. They are of that generation. Brenda probably knew little or nothing about Canadian politics or Aboriginal issues, though nobody could apologize like her.

I know a lot of people who were a little cynical about the sincerity of the apology. That is their right. If an abusive husband apologizes to his abused wife and kids, however sincere it might sound, some may doubt the authenticity of that apology. Same as in this situation, an admission of responsibility is as good a place as any to start. Ask any lawyer. But the healing must start somewhere.

I am very fortunate. Neither I nor any of my immediate relatives attended a residential school. Instead, we were schooled at the Mud Lake Indian Day School located directly on the Curve Lake Reserve in eastern Ontario. Still, many of the residential school policies extended to the communities. My mother tells of not being allowed to speak Anishnawbe on school grounds, which were located just a few hundred metres from where she lived. Just the other night, I heard her reminiscing with one of her sisters about how they made sure they never played under the windows of the school so the teacher would not hear them speaking in Anishnawbe. One usually does not think of one's seventy-seven-year old shy mother as a rebel. Maybe that is why Anishnawbe is still her first language and English a distant second.

There is a lot of collateral damage from that era as well. Hot on the heels of residential school Survivors are those who went through the Sixties Scoop, where Aboriginal kids were taken away by various social services and farmed out for adoption, usually to white families, sometimes to Europe and to the United States. They were part of the same larger, overall policy of eliminating Aboriginal culture by wiping away the memories and heritage of Aboriginal children and Canadianizing them. If you cannot get them through the front door, try the back, or even the window.

Interestingly, many Aboriginal people watching the historic *aabwehyehnmigziwin* were not actual students of residential schools. But I think it is safe to say that they were all affected by the practice in some way. Most Aboriginal people who watched knew somebody or several somebodies who attended residential school or were descended from, or a relative of, a Survivor. As a result, they were forced to deal with the repercussions of that experience. It now permeates our culture. Harper and Canada's apology was for all of us—those who attended the schools and those who are living with the fallout. Just as all Jewish people were affected by the Holocaust in some way (if I may be allowed to say this), all Aboriginal people were victims of what happened in those institutions. It is collateral damage in sort of an intergenerational way.

What happens now? I do not know. Maybe Phil Fontaine and the gang should contact Maher Arar. He might have some suggestions. If memory serves me correctly, Mr. Arar was kidnapped suddenly for no logical reason, taken far away from his family for a long period of time, beaten, starved, and terrified for the greater good. He finally returned to his family a changed man and is now seeking justice. Geez, you would think he was an Aboriginal kid or something.

As the similarly sympathetic Connie Francis who, like Brenda Lee, was neither Aboriginal nor a residential school Survivor, also sang many years ago, "I'm sorry I made you cry." Did Harper get his words right (that were chosen for him by lawyers)? Harper had said, "We are sorry... We apologize for having done this." He must not forget that there is still a Canadian issue here that all Canadians need to address as part of an ongoing relationship. Closing the book on residential schools does not mean that the "Aboriginal problem" has been solved—at least not in the eyes of the government. Thus, I will let Connie Francis finish with her poignant lyrics:

> I'm sorry I made you cry
>
> Won't you forget, won't you forgive
>
> Don't let us say goodbye

I'm just glad Harper did not try to sing the *aabwehyehnmigziwin*.

Notes

1 See pages 235-237, this volume.

2 For a brief review on the history of the Chinese head tax, please see pages 238–239 of Bradford W. Morse's article "Reconciliation Possible? Reparations Essential" in Castellano, Marlene Brant, Linda Archibald, and Mike DeGagné (2008). *From Truth to Reconciliation: Transforming the Legacy of Residential Schools.* Ottawa, ON: Aboriginal Healing Foundation: 233–256.

3 Government of Canada (1998). *Statement of Reconciliation.* Ottawa, ON: Indian and Northern Affairs Canada. Presented on 7 January 1998 by The Honourable Jane Stewart, Minister of Indian and Northern Affairs Canada. Retrieved 15 September 2008 from: http://www.ainc-inac.gc.ca/gs/rec_e.html

4 Indian and Northern Affairs Canada (no date). Indian Residential Schools Resolution Canada 2007-2008 Departmental Performance Report. Retrieved 31 March 2009 from: http://www.tbs-sct.gc.ca/dpr-rmr/2007-2008/inst/ira/ira-eng.pdf

5 See: Bowlus, Audra, Katherine McKenna, Tanis Day and David Wright (2003). *The Economic Costs and Consequences of Child Abuse in Canada.* Ottawa, ON: The Law Commission of Canada; and Native Counselling Services of Alberta (2001). *A Cost-Benefit Analysis of Hollow Water's Community Holistic Circle Healing Process.* Ottawa, ON: Solicitor General Canada and Aboriginal Healing Foundation.

6 For a brief review on the apology and redress to Japanese Canadians, please see pages 237–238 of Bradford W. Morse's article "Reconciliation Possible? Reparations Essential" in Castellano, Marlene Brant, Linda Archibald, and Mike DeGagné (2008). *From Truth to Reconciliation: Transforming the Legacy of Residential Schools.* Ottawa, ON: Aboriginal Healing Foundation: 233–256.

Biography

Drew Hayden Taylor is an award-winning playwright, author, columnist, filmmaker, and lecturer. Originally from Curve Lake First Nation (Ojibway) in central Ontario, he has spent the last two decades travelling the world spreading the gospel of First Nations literature. Drew writes about his travels from an Aboriginal perspective and manages to bridge the gap between cultures by tickling the funny bone.

During the last 25 years, Drew has done many things during his literary career, from performing stand-up comedy at the Kennedy Center in Washington D.C. to lecturing at the British Museum on the films of Sherman Alexie. Over the last two decades, he has written award-winning plays (resulting in 70-plus productions of his work); writes a column in five newspapers across the country, short stories, novels, and scripts for *The Beachcombers*, *Street Legal*, *North of Sixty*, and currently, he is the head writer for the APTN comedy series *Mixed Blessings*. He has also worked on 17 documentaries exploring the First Nations experience; most notably, he wrote and directed *Redskins, Tricksters*, and *Puppy Stew!* a documentary on First Nations humour for the National Film Board of Canada. In addition, he is also former Artistic Director of Canada's premiere Native theatre company, Native Earth Performing Arts.

Drew was the artist/writer-in-residence at the University of Michigan (2006) and the University of Western Ontario (2007). He has written and edited over 20 fiction and non-fiction books, including recently published *The Night Wanderer: A Native Gothic Novel* and *Me Sexy*, a follow-up to his highly successful non-fiction book on First Nations humour, *Me Funny*.

Boys from the Spanish Indian Residential School
Courtesy of Father William Maurice, S.J. Collection—The Shingwauk Project

Richard Wagamese

Returning to Harmony

I am a victim of Canada's residential school system. When
I say victim, I mean something substantially different than
"Survivor." I never attended a residential school, so I cannot say
that I survived one. However, my parents and my extended family members did. The pain they endured became my pain, and I
became a victim.

When I was born, my family still lived the seasonal nomadic
life of traditional Ojibwa people. In the great rolling territories
surrounding the Winnipeg River in Northwestern Ontario, they
fished, hunted, and trapped. Their years were marked by the
peregrinations of a people guided by the motions and turns of
the land. I came into the world and lived in a canvas army tent
hung from a spruce bough frame as my first home. The first
sounds I heard were the calls of loon, the snap and crackle of a
fire, and the low, rolling undulation of Ojibwa talk.

We lived communally. Along with my mother and siblings, there
were my matriarchal grandparents, aunts, uncles, and cousins.
Surrounded by the rough and tangle of the Canadian Shield, we

moved through the seasons. Time was irrelevant in the face of ancient cultural ways that we followed.

But there was a spectre in our midst.

All the members of my family attended residential school. They returned to the land bearing psychological, emotional, spiritual, and physical burdens that haunted them. Even my mother, despite staunch declarations that she had learned good things there (finding Jesus, learning to keep a house, the gospel), carried wounds she could not voice. Each of them had experienced an institution that tried to scrape the Indian off of their insides, and they came back to the bush and river raw, sore, and aching. The pain they bore was invisible and unspoken. It seeped into their spirit, oozing its poison and blinding them from the incredible healing properties within their Indian ways.

For a time, the proximity to family and the land acted as a balm. Then, slowly and irrevocably, the spectre that followed them back from the schools began to assert its presence and shunt for space around our communal fire. When the vitriolic stew of unspoken words, feelings, and memories of their great dislocation, hurt, and isolation began to bubble and churn within them, they discovered that alcohol could numb them from it. And we ceased to be a family.

Instead, the adults of my Ojibwa family became frightened children. The trauma that had been visited upon them reduced them to that. They huddled against a darkness from where vague shapes whispered threats and from where invasions of their minds, spirits, and bodies roared through the blackness to envelope and smother them again. They forgot who they were. They struck back vengefully, bitterly, and blindly as only hurt and frightened children could do.

When I was a toddler, my left arm and shoulder were smashed. Left untreated, my arm hung backwards in its joint and, over time, it atrophied and withered. My siblings and I endured great tides of violence and abuse from the drunken adults. We were beaten, nearly drowned, and terrorized. We took to hiding in the bush and waited until the shouting, cursing, and drinking died away. Those nights were cold and terrifying. In the dim light of dawn, the eldest of us would sneak back into camp to get food and blankets.

In the mid-winter of 1958, when I was almost three, the adults left my two brothers, sister, and me alone in the bush camp across the bay from the tiny railroad town of Minaki. It was February. The wind was blowing bitterly and the firewood ran out at the same time as the food. They were gone for days, drinking in Kenora sixty miles away. When it became apparent that we would freeze to death without wood, my eldest sister and brother hauled my brother, Charles, and me across the bay on a sled piled with furs.

They pulled us across that ice in a raging snowstorm. We huddled in the furs on the leeward side of the railroad depot cold, hungry, and crying. A passing Ontario provincial policeman found us and took us to the Children's Aid Society. I would not see my mother or my extended family again for twenty-one years.

I lived in two foster homes until I was adopted at age nine. I left that home at age sixteen; I ran for my safety, my security, and my sanity. The seven years I spent in that adopted home were filled with beatings, mental and emotional abuse, and a complete dislocation and disassociation from anything Indian or Ojibwa. I was permitted only the strict Presbyterian ethic of that household. It was as much an institutional kidnapping as a residential school.

For years after, I lived on the street or in prison. I became a drug user and an alcoholic. I drifted through unfulfilled relationships. I was haunted by fears and memories. I carried the residual trauma of my toddler years and the seven years in my adopted home. This caused me to experience post-traumatic stress disorder, which severely affected the way I lived my life and the choices I would make.

The truth of my life is that I am an intergenerational victim of residential schools. Everything I endured until I found healing was a result of the effects of those schools. I did not hug my mother until I was twenty-five. I did not speak my first Ojibwa word or set foot on my traditional territory until I was twenty-six. I did not know that I had a family, a history, a culture, a source for spirituality, a cosmology, or a traditional way of living. I had no awareness that I belonged somewhere. I grew up ashamed of my Native identity and the fact that I knew nothing about it. I was angry that there was no one to tell me who I was or where I had come from.

My brother Charles tracked me down with the help of a social worker friend when I was twenty-five. From there, I returned to the land of my people as a stranger knowing nothing of their experience or their pain. When I rejoined my people and learned about Canada's residential school policy, I was enraged. Their political and social history impelled me to find work as a reporter with a Native newspaper. As a writer and a journalist, I spoke to hundreds of residential school Survivors. The stories they told, coupled with my family's complete and utter reticence, told me a great deal about how my family had suffered. I knew that those schools were responsible for my displacement, my angst, and my cultural *lostness*.

For years I carried simmering anger and resentment. The more I learned about the implementation of that policy and how it affected Aboriginal people across the country, the more anger I felt. I ascribed all my pain to residential schools and to those responsible. I blamed churches for my alcoholism, loneliness, shame, fear, inadequacy, and failures. In my mind I envisaged a world where I had grown up as a fully functioning Ojibwa, and it glittered in comparison to the pain-wracked life I had lived.

But when I was in my late forties, I had enough of the anger. I was tired of being drunk and blaming the residential schools and those responsible. I was tired of fighting against something that could not be touched, addressed, or confronted. My life was slipping away on me and I did not want to become an older person still clinging to a disempowering emotion like the anger I carried.

So one day I decided that I would visit a church. Churches had been the seed of my anger. I had religion forced on me in my adopted home and it was the churches that had run the residential schools that shredded the spirit of my family. If I were to lose my anger, I needed to face the root of it squarely. I was determined that I would take myself there and sit and listen to the service. As much as I knew that I would want to walk out and as much as my anger would direct me to reject it all, I would force myself to sit and listen and try to find something that I could relate to. I chose a United Church because they had been the first to issue an apology for their role in the residential school debacle. They had been the first to publicly state their responsibility for the hurt that crippled generations. They were the first to show the courage to address wrongdoing, abuse, forced removal, and shaming. They had been the first to make tangible motions toward reconciliation. It put them in a more favourable light with me.

I was uncomfortable at first. No one spoke to me as I took my seat in a pew near the back. There were no other Native people there and I used that fact as a denunciation. When the service began, I heard everything through the tough screen of my rage. Then I noticed the old woman beside me sitting with her eyes closed as the minister spoke. She looked calm and peaceful, and there was a glow on her features that I coveted. So I closed my eyes too and tilted my head back and listened.

I ceased to hear the liturgy that day. I could not hear doctrine, semantics, proselytizations, or judgment. Instead, with my eyes closed, all I could hear was the small voice of the minister telling a story about helping a poor, drug-addicted woman on the street despite his fear and doubt. All I heard was the voice of compassion. All I heard was a spiritual, very human person talking about life and confronting its mysteries.

So I went back the next week. I went back and took my seat, and I listened with my eyes closed. After the scriptural text was read, the minister analyzed it by placing it in the context of his impatience and the lessons he had learned in the grocery line and in the freeway traffic. Here was a man responsible for directing the lives of a congregation talking about facing his own spiritual shortcomings. There was no self-aggrandization, no inferred superiority. There was only a man telling us how hard it was to behave like a spiritual being.

I went back to that church for many weeks. The messages I heard were all about humanity and about the search for innocence, comfort, and belonging. I do not know just exactly when my anger and resentment disappeared. I only know that there came a time when I could see that there was nothing in the message that was not about healing. I heard about compassion, love, kindness, trust, courage, truth, and loyalty and an abiding faith that there is a God, a Creator. There was nothing to be angry about in any of that; in fact, there was nothing different from what Native spirituality talks about. After I came home to my people I sought out teachers and healers and ceremonies. I had committed myself to learning the spiritual principles that allowed our peoples to sustain, define, and perpetuate themselves through incredible changes. I had adopted many of those teachings into my daily life, and every ceremony I attended taught me more and more about the essence of our spiritual lives. What I heard from that minister those Sunday mornings was not any different from the root message of humanity in our teachings. With my eyes closed there was no white, no Indian, no difference at all; the absence of anger happened quietly without fanfare.

It has been a few years now since I sat in that church. I have not receded back into the dark seas of resentment, rage, or old hurt. Instead, I have found a peace with churches and, in turn, with residential schools, with Canada. See, that church changed my personal politics. Sure, there are genuine reasons to be angry. The hurt caused by the residential school experience, both of the Survivors and of those like me who were victimized a generation or more later, are huge, real, and overwhelming. But healing happens if you want it bad enough, and that is the trick of it, really. Every spiritually enhancing experience asks a sacrifice of us and, in this, the price of admission is a keen desire to be rid of the block of anger.

When the Truth and Reconciliation Commission makes its tour of the country and hears the stories of people who endured the pain of residential schools, I hope it hears more stories like mine—of people who fought against the resentment, hatred, and anger and found a sense of peace. Both the Commission and Canada need to hear stories of healing instead of a relentless retelling and re-experiencing of pain. They need to hear that, despite everything, every horror, it is possible to move forward and to learn how to leave hurt behind. Our neighbours in this country need to hear stories about our capacity for forgiveness, for self-examination, for compassion, and for our yearning for peace because they speak to our resiliency as a people. That is how reconciliation happens.

It is a big word, *reconciliation*. Quite simply, it means to create harmony. You create harmony with truth and you build truth out of humility. That is spiritual. That is truth. That is Indian. Within us, as nations of Aboriginal people and as individual members of those nations, we have an incredible capacity for survival, endurance, and forgiveness. In the reconciliation with ourselves first, we find the ability to create harmony with others, and that is where it has to start—in the fertile soil of our own hearts, minds, and spirits.

That, too, is Indian.

Biography

Richard Wagamese is an Ojibway from the Wabasseemoong First Nation in northwestern Ontario. He has been a lecturer in creative writing with the University of Regina's Saskatchewan Indian Federated College, a writer for the Royal Commission on Aboriginal Peoples, a faculty advisor on journalism for Grant MacEwen Community College and the Southern Alberta Institute of Technology (SAIT), and a scriptwriter for the CBC-Alliance production *North of 60*. Recognized for his free-flowing style, Richard has been a book, film, and music reviewer, general reporter, and feature writer for numerous newspapers and journals across Canada. He has also worked extensively in both radio and television news and documentary.

Following a distinguished journalism career in which he became the first Aboriginal in Canada to win a National Newspaper Award for column writing, he moved into the realm of fiction writing. The result was the award-winning bestseller *Keeper'n Me* (1994), followed by an anthology of his newspaper columns, *The Terrible Summer* (1996), his second novel, *A Quality of Light* (1997), a memoir entitled *For Joshua: An Ojibway Father Teaches His Son* (2002), his third novel *Dream Wheels* (2006), his fourth, *Ragged Company* (2007), and finally his latest book, his second memoir, *One Native Life* (2008). Richard has been listed in *Canadian Who's Who*.

New arrivals at Moose Fort Indian Residential School
Moose Factory, Ontario
Courtesy of Janice Longboat

Sophie Pierre *née* Eustace

The Little Girl Who Would be Chief

On 22 January 2003, I stood on the front steps of the St. Eugene Mission Resort (now the St. Eugene Golf Resort & Casino), near Cranbrook, British Columbia, and proudly watched as my five year-old granddaughter, Samantha, helped cut the ribbon to officially open our hotel. As I had looked out across the snowy driveway, my mind had drifted back in time to 1956, and I saw another little girl coming up the same driveway, desperately holding on to her mother's hand and looking up towards the Sister standing on the same spot where, forty-seven years later, I stood in 2003. That little girl was me. My name is Sophie Pierre, née Eustace, a member of the Ktunaxa Nation. I am Chief of my community, Aqam, also known as St. Mary's Indian Reserve, and I am a Survivor of residential school. That little girl in 1956 would spend nine years at the Kootenay Indian Residential School and, forty-seven years later, would witness the opening of a five-star hotel at the same site. This is our story. It is a story of making the choice to turn something so negative in our history, as Ktunaxa living in our traditional territory, into something positive for our future generations. It is a story of courage, perseverance, and some might say stubborn determination, but mostly it is a story of vision and choices.

The Kootenay Indian Residential School, formerly known as the Industrial School, was built in 1910 and operated by the Catholic Church until 1970. Children from southern Alberta, the Okanagan and Shuswap, as well as from the local Ktunaxa area were brought to this school for ten months of each year. I am often asked what it was like in the school, and I reply that it was a very lonely place for a child to grow up. It did not matter if you were a local kid like me who could see my home from the top dormitory windows, but could not return there, or if you were an Okanagan or Shuswap kid who would not see their parents or their home for the whole ten months. When the school shut down in 1970, the Oblates, the priests who operated the school, made a deal with the federal government to turn over the school buildings and the land in trust to the five local bands. It seemed like a wonderful idea at the time, and the transfer was made. Before long, it became clear that what we had was, in fact, a huge white elephant. The building maintenance costs were prohibitive, and eventually the building was abandoned.

It would stand empty for the next twenty years, a constant reminder of the pain, failure, and abandonment that our people felt, until one day, at a band meeting in our community, which we call, *Aqam*, complaints were voiced about how much we had suffered and lost at the former residential school. One of our Elders, Mary Paul, very softly said, "If you think you lost so much in that building, it's not lost, you just need the courage to go back in there and get it. You only really lose something if you refuse to pick it up again." It would take a few more years of struggling with the aftermath of the residential school before we really understood what she said and then make the choice to follow her words.

Our Ktunaxa Nation Council, made up of five local bands, agreed that if we were going to do anything with the former school building it would have to be some type of a business venture, something that would generate money for its own maintenance costs. This eliminated any social program-type initiative in education or health, for example. So the idea of a hotel and golf course was born. We started talking to various people in government, like Indian and Northern Affairs Canada (INAC), in banks, and in the hospitality industry. Understandably, we were met with a fair amount of skepticism: Would anyone want to stay at a former residential school? How will we attract business being off the beaten track (meaning on the rez and away from a major highway)? How will financing be realized (again, because we are on the rez)? But we also had support right from the start by people who could see our vision, people like then premier of British Columbia, Mike Harcourt. At a business summit in London, England, Harcourt spoke of the growing business opportunities with First Nations and used our development plan as an example. Mike Harcourt remains one of our staunchest supporters to this day.

One of the first things we had to do was get the support of all our communities, since the lands where the resort was planned upon was Indian reserve lands held in common by our five bands. INAC's regulations require a referendum for any land-use development. We spent two years planning the development and bringing the plans to band meetings, to individual homes, and to any gathering we could to get as much input as possible from our nation members. This was not an easy process. There were many former students who strongly believed that we should just knock the building down—get it off the face of the earth—because they had suffered so much in that building. But slowly, primarily through the work of our youth, as they were the ones bringing the plans out to the communities, the words of Mary Paul started to come through. The referendum vote went through the five communities with no problem in 1996, and, more importantly, we had gained the approval and support of our people that would see us through the tough times ahead.

We ended up building a forty million dollar resort by creating partnerships between our tribal council and such entities as the Royal Bank, Columbia Basin Trust, Lake City Casinos, and Delta Hotels with the help of government programs like INAC's Aboriginal Business Canada Program and from Western Economic Diversification Canada and with the help of Human Resources and Social Development Canada, among others. But first we had to convince every one of these parties of our vision: to change something so negative for our people into something positive, something we could all be proud of and want to be a part of. We could only do that because we, the Ktunaxa, believed it ourselves.

In March of 2003, we had our initial nation meeting in our new hotel. This was very emotional for us as it was the first time for many of our members to re-enter the former school building. It was imperative that we were prepared for this. In the mid-nineties, our treatment centre had created an innovative program called the Residential School Trauma Training Program. This enabled members from our nation to understand the very deep-rooted effects of our residential school experience and that it was so powerful it created trauma in our lives and in the lives of all our families. I cannot possibly explain in full how critical the work was that these courageous people undertook. They first had to deal with their own pain by understanding where it came from and then they had to learn how to help themselves and then all the others out there who were still suffering. They became our Trauma Training Counsellors, and they were there to help us as we participated in our first meeting in our own hotel. The counsellors held talking circles to give everyone a chance to express their feelings and emotions. The one I participated in included many people that I had gone to school with. One woman's comments in particular stayed with me. She said, "I was really scared to come here and almost stayed home this morning, but then I remembered Mary's words and so I came. I'm so glad I did. When I came in the front door I was blown away by how beautiful the room was. It really is a hotel. It really is ours and I'm so proud of what we've done!" Both of us cried after she spoke.

The Trauma Training Counsellors did so much to make our dream a reality. While I have been given a lot of credit for the physical building of the resort, it was really these people who brought us through it safely, and they continue today to provide guidance to those still dealing with the residual effects. They also helped Survivors from other nations who came to the building while we were in the middle of the development to deal with their own ghosts. We held many cleansing ceremonies, including one with the Catholic Church—a bishop had participated. The ceremonies held both our own Ktunaxa cleansing as well as the other First Nations' cleansing ceremonies, and these were of major importance to all of us, particularly while we were doing the non-structural demolition. The majority of that work was done by our own people, and we had to ensure their safety in every sense of the word.

The 2003 year was a very challenging year, with huge ups and downs for us. With the tremendous high of seeing our dream come to fruition with the opening of the hotel came a very stressful summer of financial crisis. Even though we were in business, with the casino opening in 2002 and the golf course in its third year of operation, we were beyond broke. Every effort we made to refinance the development fell through, and by December 2003, we were seeking protection under the *Companies' Creditors Arrangement Act*,[1] one step away from bankruptcy. Because of all that we had gone through, failure was not an option. This is when our Elder's words really pulled us through; we needed courage and perseverance, especially since one of our own communities was now fighting us and insisting that we should give up and let someone else come in and take over the property. The rest of us knew we could not let that happen. So, with the full support of the other four communities, we were able to enter into a partnership with two other First Nations, Samson Cree from Alberta and Mnjikaning First

Nation from Ontario. We signed our partnership agreement in November 2004. In September 2008, we celebrated our fourth year with a positive financial report given to our shareholders at our annual meeting. This partnership, which I believe is a first between three First Nations from different parts of our country, is truly something we can all be proud of.

We chose to maintain the history of the former residential school and share it with our guests through an interpretive centre and through the many pictures we have displayed throughout the resort of our life while at the school. One of those pictures is of six little girls in their first communion finery. Sometimes, when I walk past that picture I smile at those girls and tell them, "We did ok!" You see, one of those little girls was me.

Notes

1 The *Companies' Creditors Arrangement Act* (commonly referred to as the "CCAA") is a federal Act that provides large corporations in financial trouble to restructure its financial affairs in order to avoid bankruptcy.

Biography

Sophie Pierre was born in Cranbrook, British Columbia. She obtained a business administration diploma from Camosun College in Victoria on Vancouver Island. Sophie has led her own band, St. Mary's, for 30 years, with 26 of those years as Chief. She no longer functions as chief, but still demonstrates her commitment to her community through her ongoing involvement in youth activities, women's advocacy, and Elders' support.

Sophie has always been a strong advocate of economic development as a means to achieve self-determination for Aboriginal peoples. With Sophie at the helm, she demonstrated this commitment through her dogged determination in making Ktunaxa/Kinbasket Tribal Council's St. Eugene Mission Resort a reality for her people. Her business savvy has made her one of the most recognized Aboriginal leaders in the country, and she is a frequent speaker at business and economic development conferences. In 2003, Sophie was honoured with the National Aboriginal Achievement Award in the business category for her leadership in the creation of the largest and most elegant destination resort/casino in Western Canada. "It's not a personal award," Sophie says, "It's an indication of what our bands have accomplished." In addition to this award, she was recognized as CANDO's 2002 Individual Economic Developer of the Year.

She is a past co-chair of the First Nations Summit and a recipient of the Order of British Columbia. In December 2002, Sophie received the Queen's Golden Jubilee commemorative medal, created by the Department of Canadian Heritage where recipients are nominated and selected by their hometown communities.

Mitch Miyagawa

A Sorry State

[A version of this article was published in 2009 in *The Walrus* 6 (10): 22–30.]

The government of Canada gave my family our first apology, for the internment of Japanese Canadians during World War II, in 1988. I was seventeen, and I don't remember any of it. I had other things to worry about. My mom had just left my dad, Bob Miyagawa. She'd cried and said sorry as my brother and I helped her load her furniture into the back of a borrowed pick-up. Her departure had been coming for a while. At my dad's retirement dinner the year before, his boss at the Alberta Forest Service had handed him a silver-plated pulaski, a stuffed Bertie the Fire Beaver, and a rocking chair. My mom, Carol—barely forty years old and chafing for new adventures—took one look at the rocking chair and knew the end was near.

Three months after she left, on September 22, Brian Mulroney rose to his feet in the House of Commons. The gallery was packed with Japanese Canadian seniors and community leaders, who stood as the prime minister began to speak. "The Government of Canada wrongfully incarcerated, seized the property, and disenfranchised thousands of citizens of Japanese ancestry," he intoned. "Apologies are the only way we can cleanse the past." When he finished, the gallery cheered, in a most un–Japanese Canadian defiance of parliamentary rules.

The clouds may have suddenly parted in Ottawa; the cherry blossoms in Vancouver may have spontaneously bloomed. I missed it all. It was graduation year. Every day after school, I worked at West Edmonton Mall, diving elbow deep in Quarterback Crunch ice cream so I could save up for a pool table. Weekends, I visited my mom at her new place, a small apartment within walking distance of the tracks by Stony Plain Road.

Up until then, and perhaps to this day, being half Japanese had just been something I used to make myself unique. A conversation starter. A line for picking up girls. The internment my dad and 22,000 others like him suffered was something to add to the story. It increased the inherited martyr value.

I didn't get many dates.

Four years earlier, when Brian Mulroney was leader of the Opposition, he'd asked Pierre Trudeau to apologize to Japanese Canadians. Exasperated, Trudeau shot back, "How many other historical wrongs would have to be righted?" It was Trudeau's last day in Parliament as prime minister. He finished his retort with righteous indignation: "I do not think it is the purpose of a government to right the past. I cannot rewrite history."

Trudeau must have known that the apology door, once opened, would never be closed. Mulroney might have known, too. Redress for Japanese Canadians was the beginning of our national experiment with institutional remorse—an experiment that has grown greatly over the past twenty years, intertwining itself with my family's story.

I like to look at the glass as half full: my parents' divorce was not so much a split as an expansion. They both remarried, so my kids now have more grandparents than they can count. And I've gained the most apologized-to family in the country—maybe the world.

I watched Stephen Harper's apology for Indian residential schools with my dad's wife, Etheline, on a hot night in the summer of 2008. Etheline was the third generation of her Cree family to attend an Indian mission school. She went to Gordon Residential School in Punnichy, Saskatchewan, for four years. Gordon was the last federally run residential school to be closed, shutting down in 1996 after over a century in operation.

When I talked to my mom in Calgary afterward, she casually mentioned that her second husband, Harvey's father, had paid the Chinese head tax as a child. Harper apologized to head tax payers and their families in 2006.

I was aware that my family had become a multi-culti case study, but when I realized the government had apologized to us three times it went from being a strange coincidence to a kind of joke.

(*Q: How does a Canadian say hello? A: "I'm sorry."*) Soon, though, I started wondering what these apologies really meant, and whether they actually did any good. In seeking answers, I've mostly found more questions. I've become both a cynic and a believer. In other words, I'm more confused than ever before. I'm no apology expert or prophet. I'm so sorry. All I can offer is this: my apology story.

In the fall of 2008, I travelled from my home in Whitehorse to Vancouver. The National Association of Japanese Canadians had organized a celebration and conference on the twentieth anniversary of Redress. It rained as I walked to toward the Japanese Hall on Alexander Street in East Vancouver, in what was once the heart of the Japanese community. In the distance, giant red quay cranes poked above the buildings along Hastings, plucking containers from cargo ships anchored in Burrard Inlet. The downpour soaked the broken folks lined up outside the Union Gospel Mission at Princess and Cordova, a few blocks from the hall. Some huddled under the old cherry trees in Oppenheimer Park, beside the ball field where the Asahi baseball team, the darlings of "Japantown," played before the war.

Inside the hall, a few hundred people milled about, drinking green tea and coffee served from big silver urns by bluevested volunteers. The participants on the first panel of the day, titled Never Too Late, took seats on the wide stage at the front. They represented the hyphenated and dual named of our country: a Japanese-, Chinese-, Indo-, Black, Aboriginal, and Ukrainian-Canadian rainbow behind two long fold-out tables. Their communities had all been interned, or excluded, or systematically mistreated. Apology receivers and apology seekers. A kick line of indignation, a gallery of the once wronged. *(A Japanese-, Chinese-, Indo-, Black, Aboriginal, and Ukrainian-Canadian all go into a bar. The bartender looks at them and says, "Is this some kind of joke?")*

In the fictional world of *Eating Crow*, a "novel of apology" by Jay Rayner, the hottest trend in international relations is something called "penitential engagement." To deal with the baggage from the wars, genocides, and persecutions of the past, the United Nations sets up an Office of Apology. The protagonist of the novel, Marc Basset, is hired as Chief Apologist, partly because of his tremendous ability to deliver heartfelt apologies, but also because of his "plausible apologibility." His ancestors captained slave ships, ran colonies, slaughtered natives, and waged dirty wars. Backed by a team of researchers and handlers, Basset circles the globe, delivering statements of remorse.

Penitential engagement is closer to reality than you'd think. The Japanese government has made at least forty "war apology statements" since 1950. All of Western Europe remembers German chancellor Willy Brandt's famous *Kniefall* in 1970, when he fell to his knees on the steps of the Warsaw Memorial, in silent anguish for the victims of the Warsaw Ghetto uprising. During the past twenty years, Italian prime minister Silvio Berlusconi has apologized for the colonial occupation of Libya, South African president Frederik W. de Klerk has apologized for apartheid, and the Queen has issued a Royal Proclamation of regret to the Acadians in the Maritimes and Louisiana. In 1998, the Australian government began its annual National Sorry Day for the "stolen generations" of aboriginal children. In 2005, the US Senate apologized for its failure to enact federal anti-lynching legislation. And both houses of Congress have now passed apologies for slavery.

At the 2001 UN World Conference against Racism, Racial Discrimination, Xenophobia and Related Intolerance, held in Durban, more than 100 countries called "on all those who have not yet contributed to restoring the dignity of the victims to find appropriate ways to do so and, to this end, appreciate those countries that have done so." Working toward this goal is the International Center for Transitional Justice in New York, which "assists countries pursuing accountability for past mass atrocity or human rights abuse." As if in response, jurisdictions across Australia, the United States, and Canada are passing apology acts designed to allow public officials to apologize without incurring legal liability.

Concerned about our precious self-image as a peacemaking, multicultural country, Canada has been making every effort to lead the sorry parade. In addition to the residential school and Chinese head tax apologies, the federal government has also now said sorry for the *Komagata Maru* incident, when a ship full of immigrants from India was turned away from Vancouver Harbour, and established a historical recognition program "to recognize and commemorate the historical experiences and contributions of ethno-cultural communities affected by wartime measures and immigration restrictions applied in Canada." And we became the first Western democracy to follow South Africa in establishing a truth and reconciliation commission, for the residential schools.

Not surprisingly, other groups have come knocking on Ottawa's door. Among them are Ukrainian Canadians, on behalf of those interned during World War I, and the residents of the bulldozed Africville community in Halifax, now a dog park. Some who have already received an apology clamour for more, or better. Harper's *Komagata Maru* apology was issued to the Indo-Canadian community outside Parliament. Now they want the same as every other group: an official, on-the-record statement.

I sat down on a plastic-backed chair in the deserted second row. Seconds later, an old *Nisei*, a second-generation Japanese Canadian named Jack Nagai, plunked down beside me. He sighed and lifted the glasses hanging around his neck to his face. "Gotta sit close for my hearing aid," he said, then looked at me and grinned. I pulled out a notebook, and he watched me out of the corner of his eye, fingering the pen in his breast pocket.

Black scuffs, I wrote. The pearly walls and floor of the Japanese Hall auditorium were marked and streaked. A fluorescent light fifteen metres above my head flickered and buzzed. The hall had a school gym wear and tear to it. Jack noticed my scribbling and jotted down something on the back of his program.

The brown spots on his bald head reminded me of my Uncle Jiro, who passed away suddenly in 2005 at the age of seventy-seven. As it turned out, Jack was from Lethbridge as well, and had known my uncle from the city's Buddhist Church. My Uncle Jiro, "Jerry" to his non-Japanese friends, had helped the blind to read, bowled every Sunday, and kept a meticulous journal of the prices he'd paid for groceries and the sorry state of his golf game. He'd been a bachelor, mateless and childless, like several others on my dad's side.

Those few of us in my family who now have kids have Caucasian spouses, so our strain is becoming less and less Asian. The Miyagawa name may disappear here with my two sons, and with the name would go a story seeded a hundred years ago.

My grandmother and grandfather farmed berries on three hectares of rocky slope in Mission, BC, starting in the 1920s. They were their own slave-drivers, labouring non-stop to clear the land and get the farm going. Grandmother produced the workforce, delivering a baby a year for a decade. My dad was near the end, the ninth child of ten. By 1941, the Japanese controlled the berry industry in BC. My grandparents' farm expanded and flourished.

Then came Pearl Harbor, war with Japan, and the dislocation of more than 20,000 Japanese Canadians from the West Coast. On a spring day in 1942, my dad and his family carried two bags each to the station and boarded a train bound for the sugar beet fields of southern Alberta. They never made it back to Mission. The Japanese Canadians weren't allowed to return to BC until four years after the war was over, so the family instead settled in Lethbridge. Dad moved away soon after he came of age, and ended up in Edmonton, where I was born.

For my dad, the apology was pointless. Like many others in the Japanese Canadian community, he had already turned the other cheek. *Shikata ga nai*, the saying goes—what's done is done.

I admire and marvel at his ability to let go of the past. He even calls his family's forced move across the Rockies a "great adventure." For a ten-year-old, it was a thrill to see the black smoke pouring from the train engine's stack as it approached the Mission station.

Mist softens a train platform in the Fraser Valley. Last night's rain drips from the eaves of the station, clinging to the long tips of cedar needles. All over the platform, families are huddled together by ramshackle pyramids of suitcases. Children squat around a puddle on the tracks, poking at a struggling beetle with a stick. A distant whistle; their mother yells at them in Japanese; they run back to stand beside her. Their father stands apart, lost in thought. He's trying to commit to memory the place where he'd buried his family's dishes the night before, in one of his berry fields a few kilometres away.

Clickety-clack. Clickety-clack. A screech of brakes, a sizzle of steam. The train pulls in, the doors open, each one sentinelled by a Mountie with arms crossed.

The families become mist, along with their suitcases and the Mounties. Everything disappears except the train. It's quiet. An old conductor in a blue cap sticks his head out the window. No need for tickets on this train, he says. Step right up. Welcome aboard the Apology Express.

The conference began, and Jack and I leaned forward to hear. The panellists took their turns bending into low mikes, paying homage to the hallowed ground zero of apologies. Chief Robert Joseph, a great bear of a man in a red fleece vest, hugged the podium and said, "The Japanese Canadian apology was a beacon." Everyone at the tables looked tiny, posed between the high black skirting framing the stage and the minuscule disco ball that hung above them.

The people telling the stories of their communities were the same ones who had put on their best shoes to walk the marbled floors of Parliament, who had filed briefs for lawsuits. They spoke in the abstract—reconciliation, compensation, acknowledgement—and kept up official outrage as they demanded recognition for their causes. "We have to remember, so it will never happen again" was the panel's common refrain. After an hour, Jack's eyes were closed, and he'd started to lean my way. I could hear soft snoring from the other side of the room, where a group of seniors slumped and tilted in their chairs.

This wasn't what I'd come to hear either. After studying and listening to official expressions of remorse to my family and others, after reading the best books on the subject (*The Age of Apology*; *I Was Wrong*; *On Apology*; *Mea Culpa*), I'd come to believe that government apologies were more about forgetting than remembering.

I righted Jack as best I could, and snuck out the back of the hall for some fresh air.

I've always imagined that my mom met Harvey Kwan in a room full of light bulbs. They both worked for the Energy Efficiency Branch of the provincial government. She wrote copy for newsletters; he did tech support. In my mind, Mom would watch the way Harvey methodically screwed the bulbs into the bare testing socket. She appreciated his size. Not quite five feet tall, my mom likes her husbands compact (though she did dally for a time with a rather tall embezzler from Texas). She was further attracted to Harvey's quiet voice, his shy smile as he explained wattages and life cycles. Perhaps they reached for the same compact fluorescent and felt a jolt as their fingers touched.

Mom and "Uncle Harv" were both laid off soon after they started dating, so they moved from Edmonton to Calgary, closer to their beloved Rockies, and became true weekend warriors, driving past the indifferent elk on Highway 1 to Canmore and Banff to hike and camp and ski. Mom was afraid of heights; Harv took her hand and led her to the mountaintops.

Harvey's father had sailed to Canada aboard the *Empress of Russia* in 1919, at the age of fourteen. He paid the $500 head tax, then rode the CPR with his father to the railroad town of Medicine Hat, on the hot, dry Alberta prairie. Around the time he became an adult, in 1923, the Canadian government passed a *Chinese Immigration Act*, which remained in force for twenty-five years. Under the act, no new Chinese immigrants could come to Canada, so a young bachelor like him could only have a long-distance family. He managed to sire three sons with his first wife in China during that time, but she never made it to Canada, dying overseas. He eventually took a second wife, Harvey's mom, who had to wait several years before she could enter the country. In the meantime, she lived unhappily with Harvey's father's mother, probably waiting on her like a servant.

And that's all Harvey knows. He doesn't know about his father's life, those twenty-five years away from his first wife and their children, then his second. He doesn't know his grandfather's name. He doesn't know what his grandfather did. He doesn't know where the man is buried. They never spoke of that time.

> Mr. Speaker, on behalf of all Canadians and the Government of Canada, we offer a full apology to Chinese Canadians for the head tax and express our deepest sorrow for the subsequent exclusion of Chinese immigrants... No country is perfect. Like all countries, Canada has made mistakes in its past, and we realize that. Canadians, however, are a good and just people, acting when we've committed wrong. And even though the head tax—a product of a profoundly different time—lies far in our past, we feel compelled to right this

historic wrong for the simple reason that it is the decent thing
to do, a characteristic to be found at the core of the Canadian
soul.—*Stephen Harper, June 22, 2006*

Apology comes from the Greek *apo* and *logos* ("from speech"),
and as every first-year philosophy student who reads Plato's
Apology knows, it originally meant a defence of one's position.
But somewhere along the line, it became a Janus word, adopting
its opposite meaning as well. Rather than a justification of one's
position or actions, it became an admission of harm done, an
acceptance of responsibility. When Harper spoke on the head
tax, you could see both faces of the word at work: *Those were
different times. We're not like that now. We should, in fact,
be proud of ourselves. Pat ourselves on the back. Reaffirm
our goodness today by sacrificing the dead and gone.*

Rather than bringing the past to life, statements like these seem
to break our link with history, separating us from who we were
and promoting the notion of our moral advancement. They also
whitewash the ways in which Canadians still benefit from that
past, stripping the apologies of remorse. Rendering them meaningless. Forgettable.

I wasn't the only one taking a break from the conference. I followed a Japanese Canadian woman with short grey hair down
the street to Oppenheimer Park, watching from a distance
as she placed her hand, gently, on the trunk of one of the old
cherry trees. I later learned that these were memorial trees,
planted by Japanese Canadians thirty years ago. The City of

Vancouver had been planning to chop them down as part of a recent redevelopment scheme, but the Japanese Canadian community rallied and saved them (though the old baseball diamond will still be plowed under).

I arrived back at the hall in time for lunch. Ahead of me in line was the author and scholar Roy Miki, one of the leading figures in the movement for Japanese Canadian redress and a member of the negotiating committee for the National Association of Japanese Canadians. Miki was an "internment baby," born in Manitoba in 1942, six months after his family was uprooted from their home in Haney, BC. He laughed when I told him about my family and, intrigued, pulled up a chair beside me for lunch. He had neat white hair, parted to one side, and wore blue-tinted glasses. We balanced bento boxes on our knees, and he told me something that astounded me: the negotiators hadn't wanted an apology very badly.

"We wanted to shine a light on the system—to show its inherent flaws," he said. "Our main concern wasn't the apology or the compensation. The real victim was democracy itself, not the people." What those pushing for redress wanted was an acknowledgement that democracy had broken down, and that people had benefited from the internment of Japanese Canadians. They wanted to change the system in order to protect people in the future.

Miki remained wary of government expressions of remorse, concerned that the emotional content of apologies—the focus on "healing"—distracted from the more important issue of justice. "Now the apology has become the central thing," he said. "It allows the government to be seen as the good guy. But there's a power relationship in apologies that has to be questioned; the apologizer has more power than the apologized-to."

Mulroney, in his apology to Japanese Canadians, said the aim was "to put things right with the surviving members—with their children and ours, so that they can walk together in this country, burdened neither by the wrongs nor the grievances of previous generations." Both the victimizer and the victim are freed from their bonds. Japanese Canadian internment "went against the very nature of our country." With the apology, so the redemption narrative went, Mulroney was returning Canada to its natural, perfect state. Cue music. Roll credits. The lights come up, and all is right with the world again. I find the storyline hard to resist, especially when the main characters are long gone. But of course not all of these dramas took place once upon a time.

My dad met his second wife, Etheline Victoria Blind, at a south Edmonton bingo. Yes, he found a native bride at a bingo, in front of a glass concession case where deep-fried pieces of bannock known as "kill-me-quicks" glistened under neon light.

I was working for an environmental organization at the time. Like most Alberta non-profits, we depended on bingos and casinos as fundraisers. Dad was one of our A-list volunteers. He was retired, reliable, and always cheerful, if a bit hard of hearing. Etheline, on the other hand, was on the long-shot volunteer list. She was the mother of the high school friend of a colleague. I didn't know her, but I called her one night in desperation.

I don't remember seeing any sparks fly between Dad and Etheline. He was sixty-five at the time, and not seeking to kick at the embers of his love life. But Etheline invited him to play Scrabble with her, and so it began.

Dad and Etheline had a cantankerous sort of affair, from my point of view. They lived separately for many years—Dad in a condo on Rainbow Valley Road, Etheline in an aging split-level five minutes away—but moved gradually toward each other, in location and spirit, finally marrying a few days after Valentine's Day, eight years after they met. I flew down from Whitehorse with my son, just a year old then. He was the only person at the wedding wearing a suit, a one-piece suede tuxedo.

And so Etheline became my Indian stepmother.

Stephen Harper's apology to residential school survivors was a powerful political moment. You had to be moved by the sight of the oldest and youngest survivors, side by side on the floor of Parliament—one a 104-year-old woman, the other barely in her twenties. The speeches were superb, the optics perfect. Yet personally, I felt tricked. Tricked because the apology distilled the entire complicated history of assimilation into a single policy, collapsing it like a black hole into a two-word "problem": residential schools. Here was the forgetful apology at its best. By saying sorry for the schools, we could forget about all the other ways the system had deprived—and continued to deprive—aboriginal people of their lives and land. The government had created the problem, sure, but had owned up to it, too, and was on its way to getting it under control, starting with the survivors' prescription for recovery. If they were abused, they merely had to itemize their pain in a thirty-page document, tally their compensation points, stand before an adjudicator to speak of their rape and loneliness, and receive their official payment. All taken care of.

And yet. And yet.

Etheline, I apologize. I knew you for ten years and never really knew where you came from. I'm educated, post-colonial, postmodern, mixed race, well travelled, curious, vaguely liberal, politically correct. "You're the most Canadian person I know," I've been told. And yet I never once asked you about your time in residential school. I never really related until that night, after we'd watched Harper's shining moment, that powerful ceremony—and I'd watched how it moved you, felt the hair on my arms rise and a shiver in my back when we talked late and you told me how your grandfather was taken from his family when he was four, the same age my oldest son is now; told me how he'd never known his parents, but relearned Cree ways from his adopted family and became a strong Cree man even after his own children were taken away; how he'd raised you when your mother couldn't; how you were in the mission school, too, for four years, and your grandfather wouldn't let them cut your braids, and you'd feel the cold brick walls with your hands, and the laundry ladies would only call you by your number, and you would stare out the window toward the dirt road that led away from the school and cry for your *Kokum* and *Meshom*. I never knew. Or if you told me, I only listened with half an ear. And I apologize again, for bringing it all up, for writing down your private pain. But I know we need to tell it again and again. It has to be there; it has to get into people's hearts.

And here I make an apology for the government apology. For whatever I feel about them, about how they can bury wrongs in the past instead of making sure the past is never forgotten, about how they can use emotion to evade responsibility, they have indeed changed my life. They've made me rethink what it means to be a citizen of this country. They've brought me closer to my family.

Near the end of the conference, the woman with short grey hair stood up and told a story. After World War II, when she was a schoolgirl, she'd one day refused to read out loud from a text-book with the word "Jap" in it. She was sent home, where she proudly told her father what she'd done. He slapped her across the face. The apology, she told everyone at the hall, had restored her dignity. The conference ended the next day, and I returned home with something to think about.

It's summer as I write, almost a year since the conference, and the apologies have kept coming. The state of California apologized for the persecution of Chinese immigrants last week. Thousands of former students of Indian day schools, feeling left out of the residential school apology, filed a statement of claim at the Manitoba legislature yesterday.

I'm sitting on the beach of Long Lake, just outside Whitehorse. Though it's hot outside, the water here always stays cold, because the summer's not long enough to heat it. Still, my two boys are hardy Yukoners, and they're running in and out of the water, up to their necks. I watch their little bodies twist and turn, then look at my own thirty-eight-year-old paunch and search the sky. What will we be apologizing for when my children are adults? Temporary foreign workers? The child welfare system?

Tomio bumps into Sam, knocking him to the ground. Sam cries. "Tomio," I tell my oldest, "say sorry to your brother." "Why?" he asks. "I didn't mean to do it."

"Say sorry anyway," I reply.

We say sorry when we are responsible and when we are not. We say sorry when we were present or when we were far away. We are ambiguous about what apologies mean in the smallest personal interactions. How can we expect our political apologies to be any less complicated?

A long time ago—or not so long ago, really, but within our nation's lifetime—another train hustled along these tracks: the

Colonial Experiment. She was a beaut, shiny and tall. Ran all the way from Upper Canada; ended here in this lush Pacific rainforest. The Colonial Experiment was strictly one way, so it's up to the Apology Express to make the return trip.

Watch as we go by: a Doukhobor girl peeks out from under her house, her head scarf muddy. The police officers who took her sister and her friends away to the school in New Denver are gone and won't be back for another week. A Cree boy, hair freshly shorn into a brush cut, stares out the window of a residential school in the middle of the Saskatchewan grasslands, watching his parents' backs as they walk away. A Japanese fisherman hands over the keys to his new boat. A Ukrainian woman swats the mosquitoes away, bends to pick potatoes at Spirit Lake, and feels her baby dying inside her. A Chinese man living under a bridge thinks about his wife at home and wonders if he'll see her again.

But take heart: at every stop on the way back, someone important will say sorry for their lot. Just like the man in the top hat on my son's train engine TV show, he'll make it all better, no matter how much of a mess there's been.

All aboard. If you feel a little sick, it's just the motion of the cars. Close your eyes. Try not to forget.

Biography

Mitch Miyagawa is a writer and filmmaker from Whitehorse, Yukon. He was born and raised in Edmonton, Alberta, and moved to the Yukon in 1998, where he lives with his wife and two sons. Mitch began his writing career in 2002 with the production of his first play, *The Plum Tree*. It was produced in six cities across Canada, including at the prestigious playRites Festival in Calgary, and was published in 2004 by Playwrights Canada Press. He was the playwright-in-residence at Nakai Theatre in Whitehorse, where he wrote *Carnaval*, produced by Nakai Theatre in 2007. In film, his documentary for the National Film Board, *Our Town Faro* (2004), won the Northern Sights Competition and was nominated for a Golden Sheaf at the Yorkton Short Film Festival. He co-produced *The Lottery Ticket* (2003), an award-winning short for BravoFACT, and *Artifacts* (2007), a short drama for Haeckel Hill Pictures. He co-wrote a feature film for Force Four Films called *The Asahi Baseball Story*. He is currently in post-production on a one-hour documentary on government apologies, commissioned by TVO for their point-of-view documentary program, *The View From Here*. As a freelancer, Mitch has written for several magazines, including *Geist*, *Up Here*, *North of Ordinary*, and *The Walrus*. He won honourable mentions at both the Western and National Magazine awards for his work. He is a graduate of the Masters of Fine Arts program in Creative Writing at the University of British Columbia.

"Looking Unto Jesus." A class in penmanship at the Red Deer Indian
Industrial School, Red Deer, Alberta, ca. 1914 or 1919
Photographer: United Church of Canada
Victoria University Archives, 93.049P/850N
(Photo: Courtesy of the Legacy of Hope Foundation)

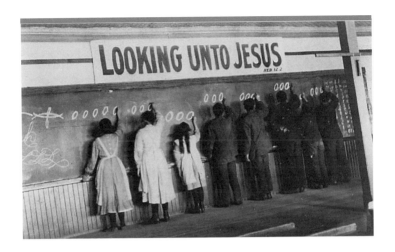

Sid Chow Tan

Aiyah![1] A Little Rouse of Time and Space

(excerpt)

Even with testimonial witness and record, historians still make educated guesses to fill in the gaps. When there are no witnesses and records to history, one can only imagine. Yet with imagination, the divination of grand meaningful historical events is possible, and the minutia within. So it is with "A Little Hoy Ping on the Prairies" and "Gim and Ruby," stories of the meeting between my Grandfather and Indigenous people in what would be his final resting place on the great plains of North America.

What follows are two tellings of the story of a seminal moment for our family. The narrative account is my response to a call for submissions for a Chinese Canadian National Council online history and culture project five years ago. The dialogic account is my ongoing personal effort, manifesting partly in Gold Mountain Turtle Island, a collaborative First Nations and Chinese opera in development by the Carnegie Community Centre in the Downtown Eastside of Vancouver, British Columbia. Both efforts are rooted in my belief that

First Nations and the Chinese in Canada must look to the future for a fair telling of their history.

There are many people to thank for their encouragement: my children and their children, their partners, the mother of my children and our grandchildren, my friends and frequent critics Anne-Marie Sleeman, Leah Kaser, Jim Wong-Chu, Victor Wong, Sean Gunn, and Elwin Xie. Special thanks to Rika Uto and Ethel Whitty of the Carnegie Community Centre, Donna Spencer of the Firehall Arts Centre, and collaborators Renae Morriseau, Michelle La Flamme, and Shon Wong of the First Nations/Chinese Opera project. For my Grandparents, Chow Gim (Norman) Tan and Wong Nooy Tan. May their sleep soothe.

1) A Little *Hoy Ping*[2] on the Prairies

Ah Yeh (paternal grandfather) had good luck. His survival in Canada came with the close friendships formed with the local Cree and Métis clans of the great plains of Gum San (Gold Mountain/North America). To these Aboriginal and Native brothers and sisters, our family thanks you.

Ah Yeh's early life in Canada was loneliness and hard work. He silently cursed the racist exclusion law (1923–1947)[3] that separated him from his new wife and recently born son. It would be a quarter of a century before he could be reunited with his wife here in Canada. Then they would wait nearly another quarter of a century before their only child and his family could join them.

Mercifully, opening and running a café supplanted the loneliness. He often thought of the money he borrowed for the head tax and starting his café. Then would silently curse again the racist law that required only Chinese people to pay a tax to come to Canada. He always wondered why he and all other Chinese were required to pay a tax that was enough to buy two houses. Europeans got free land to farm. He knew the obvious answer. Oh well, he thought, at least the government allowed him to hire Indian women to help waitress and wash dishes. A law forbade him and other Chinese business owners from hiring white women.

Every day, Ah Yeh hoped for enough business so there was money to send back to and support his family in China. The two-elevator Saskatchewan town Ah Yeh had opened shop in had an Indian Agency. This manifest of the so-called 'white man's burden' doled out ammunition, snare wire, and food vouchers for Indians living on reservations. Most of the Indian reservations were within a day's walking distance to the Post Office where the Agency was located.

A childhood playmate lived in a suite on the third floor of the town's federal and largest building because his parents did the cleaning and fixing. The boast of the town is the second oldest continuous operating courthouse in Canada built next to the historic provincial Land Titles office. Two blocks away, upstairs in the Town Hall, was reputedly the grandest opera house on the Canadian prairies when built.

Another childhood playmate lived south of us, across a vacant lot with his 'in-town' relatives. Ah Yeh eventually bought and renovated the solidly built house and also built a house on the vacant lot. My friend was a local Cree band chief's son, and we would often walk to school together in those carefree days of life. Our facial features and hair were similar and our friendship playful. This welcomed a little Hoy Ping in the territory of the mighty Cree Nation of Saskatchewan near Sweetgrass and Red Pheasant.

Ah Yeh often swapped cash for the food vouchers the Indians received. Over the years, his café slowly became both a retail store and a small wholesale food outlet to the nudge–nudge wink–wink of special redemption-for-voucher locals. During the winter, his garage behind the store was often an overnight stop for those too drunk or tired to make the long trip home to the reservation. Many hunters, Indian and whites, would bring seemingly waste parts of bears, deer, moose, and other wild animals in exchange for food and cash. Ah Yeh would dry and prepare the parts, selling them for medicinal purposes to the knowing.

Fast forward 50 years later...

When I was naughty or didn't study Chinese, Ah Yeh would call me a *mong gok doy* (lost kingdom boy), meaning the loss of country and culture. In reality, he was referring to Aboriginal people, defeated by the superior firepower, Europeans who stole their land and then tried to erase their language and culture. It was Ah Yeh's rule that my adopted brother and I had to speak Chinese in the back of the store where we ate and slept. The penalty for not speaking Chinese? A knuckle duster ring on the skull. Ouch! Ah Nging (paternal grandmother), who carried me to Canada as a baby 'paper son'—illegally—in 1950, also called me a *mong gok doy* along with expletives and endearments. Her penalty for not speaking Chinese? The ear grab. Ouch!

Ah Yeh often used the story of how young Indians lost their language and culture to try to convince my brother and me of what would befall us if we did not have Chinese reading and writing skills. My answer to his preachings? Then as now, never having been the sharpest knife in the drawer, I rebelled against his old-fashioned ideas—comics, rock and roll, and later a clandestine firecracker, condoms, and cigarettes franchise among my friends. One thing led to another—girls, cars, university, et cetera. Some Hoy Ping language survives with me though, thanks to Ah Yeh's knuckle dusting and Ah Nging's ear grabs. Ah Yeh gave Chinese names to my children, the first of our family line to be born in the Gold Mountain after a century and a half of struggle. Sadly, my grandparents did not live to see my first grandchild—the fifth generation of our Tan branch of the Chow family tree to be living in Canada.

Ah Yeh showed wisdom but was aloof, my being Ah Nging's baby Buddha. As a boy, a child really, Grandfather at age ten was already imbued with the spirit of the Kwan Kung—righteousness, devotion, and loyalty—when he offered to look after a rich man's cows so his older sister would not be sold. Whenever Ah Nging told this story, she would cry. Her husband was a man who jumped at the chance to *dow jee foo*—go to land of perpetual toil—at age nineteen. Without any classroom schooling, Ah Yeh eventually taught himself to read and write Chinese and a little bit of English too. Because he gave locals credit for food and goods, his story of times and spaces is memorable and prescient: simply, a Canada that excluded him for most of his life but within it, a people who welcomed him.

Ah Yeh explained we are the people of *jung gok*—the middle or centre kingdom. It is natural for an affinity to exist between middle and lost kingdoms, more so since both had suffered under *hun mor gok*—the kingdom of the red hairs. Now called *ying gok*, the 'red hairs' is in reference to British and white English speakers who evidently ate a lot of carrots. The Chinese 'ying' character here means 'heroic and dashing.' Hey, police then were known as *look yee*—green coats—because green was the uniform colour of immigration officials. Ah Yeh's take on the British was to adopt the name Norman because they had defeated the Anglos.

There is no written record of when the middle and lost kingdom crossed paths in historic Battleford, Saskatchewan—at one time the site of the territorial government of most of what is now western Canada. Almighty Voice is a legend here. Louis Riel had spent time in the Fort Battleford jail, as did Cree leaders Chiefs Poundmaker and Big Bear. Wandering Spirit was among the six Cree and two Assiniboine men hung for insurrection within the fort's stockade, the largest mass hanging in Canada since Confederation. Norman of the Hoy Ping clan of the middle kingdom, driven to this land by hunger, arrived to seek opportunity.

In my mind, Ah Yeh's seminal meeting with the Cree was simple, solemn, and about respect, consent, and trust. He would have introduced himself by saying he was pleased to meet the leaders of the Red Pheasant and Sweetgrass clan of the Cree people.

"Welcome to my café. My name is Norman and I am a cook. Together we can prosper so I can bring my wife and son to live among you. We have a common racist enemy so let us help each other. Like me, you do not have the vote so are treated as second class. We will talk more about this after you taste my cooking."

"Your face and words tell us you are a brother. Your offer to feed us shows you are generous and respectful. I am Len, chief of the Red Pheasant. We welcome you as our brother," says the apparent commander of the men of the Red Pheasant and Sweetgrass. He nods to those closest to the outside door, and two big tubfuls of fresh fish and game, a sack of potatoes, and a mix of vegetables are brought, deposited in the kitchen.

Norman turns the radio on and instructs the men to help themselves to coffee. Len and Norman go to the kitchen. Here Norman purposefully amazes the chief with his deftness and flourishes with axe, meat cleaver, and knife in cutting and preparing the bounty. Len asks Norman if he'll teach him how to cut and chop like him. They both begin work on the feast of fusion—likely venison chop suey, roast wild duck with potatoes, fried and steamed fresh pickerel, and goldeye. Of course there would be rice and soy sauce.

Norman's cooking is clearly a hit with the Cree men, even though they tease Len that it is women's work. When most are done eating, three young Cree women arrive with more game and potatoes. They take away the leftover food, tasting and giggling all the while clearing the tables, washing the dishes, and cleaning the kitchen. Norman seems beguiled by one woman apparently in charge, and his new Cree brothers notice. She smiles, he smiles, everyone smiles. Later, Norman lets them all know he is the sole support for his extended family in China whom he misses very much. Slowly, everyone leaves except Len.

"My sister Ruby smiles at you because she needs a job. Her husband has run off," Len says to Norman, who brings out a bottle of scotch and two glasses. Len shakes his head from side to side, lifting his coffee cup. "Whiskey poisons my people. I do not drink it. Ruby raises her son alone because her boy's father loves whiskey too much. Ruby is a good woman and does not drink whiskey anymore."

"I understand," acknowledges Norman, pouring Len another coffee and himself a three-finger drink and lighting a cigarette. "Whiskey is the small warmth at the end of a long work day. Soothing if I do not drink more than a small glass or two. Your sister is a good worker. I need help with the weekend lunch and dinner trade and will treat her fairly."

Norman ran his café and store for nearly fifty years, over twenty-five without Nooy, his wife and their son, Wing, because of Canada's racist exclusion law against us Chinese. When asked about this, he looks towards the back wall shrine of Kwan Kung, patron protector of warriors, writers, and artists, facing the front door. Then he looks upward as towards heaven and thanks the local Indians and Métis for their friendship. Ah Nging coughs. Ah Yeh then gives a thumbs up and in a warrior's voice proclaims, *"Lo wah kiu ho sai lai"*—old overseas Chinese number one.

Ah Nging chuckles saying, "Ho yeah, ho yeah"—good stuff, good stuff.

Grandfather and Grandmother, I will never forget you.

Notes

1 *Aiyah* is an exclamation in Chinese. It is used as a sigh or "oh, oh" or "wow man."

2 *"Hoy Ping"* literally means "open peace" and is the name of a district in southern China. This story was first published as an online essay at the Asian Canadian Culture Online Project website: http://www.ccnc .ca/accop/index.php?section= content/essays/essayMain.php &sub=content/essays/sidTan/ sidTan.shtml

3 See: *The Chinese Immigration Act* (1923). S.C., c. 38.

Biography

Born in China and a baby paper son (illegal) immigrant to Canada in 1950 following the repeal of Chinese exclusion, **Sid Chow Tan** is a descendant of pioneer adventurers. Raised in small-town Saskatchewan by grandparents, a graduate of the University of Calgary and nearly forty-year resident of Metro Vancouver, Sid has been active for nearly three decades in community media and redress for the Chinese head tax/exclusion laws. Growing up the youngest in the only Chinese family in town, Sid's politics is informed by a life of anti-racism and social justice activism, occasionally resulting in civil disobedience and arrest. His first recollection as an activist is a grade seven school debate supporting universal health care. Since then, he has helped found and build organizations in Vancouver and across Canada to fill community and personal needs. A freelance media producer and community organizer, Sid's current community service includes national chairman of the Chinese Canadian National Council and founding and current director of Head Tax Families Society of Canada, ACCESS Association of Chinese Canadians for Equality and Solidarity Society, National Anti-Racism Council of Canada, Downtown Eastside Community Arts Network, Downtown Eastside Neighbourhood Council, W2 Social Enterprise Café Society, CMES Community Media Education Society, and W2 Community Media Arts Society, soon to be operating a multi-purpose multi-platform media arts centre in the historic Woodward's building. Father to a son and daughter, his art is activism and his trade is in organizing.

Boys on the dock from the Spanish Indian Residential School
Courtesy of Father William Maurice, S.J. Collection – The Shingwauk
Project

Roy Miki

By Turns Poetic: Redress as Transformation (excerpt)

For Canadians of Japanese ancestry, the 22 September 1988 redress settlement with the federal government stood as the culmination of a difficult effort to resolve a complex of injustices endured in the 1940s—from mass uprooting to dispossession, internment, and, for many, the ignominy of deportation. That was the historic day when they received the long-awaited acknowledgement of the injustices, along with individual and community compensation, pardons for those wrongfully convicted, citizenship for those who had been deported as well as their children, and a public foundation to fight racism, eventually established as the Canadian Race Relations Foundation.

My account of this event in *Redress: Inside the Japanese Canadian Call for Justice* situated the redress movement in the multi-faceted interplay between the national politics of citizenship with its democratic values and the subjective spaces of memory and desire that constituted the history of Japanese Canadians (hereafter JCs), myself included, across several generations.[1] The heart-wrenching consequences of dispersal from our West Coast homes saturated the nooks and crannies of my childhood, feeding my imagination with stories of tearful separations and losses, not only of properties and belongings, but more deeply of dignity and well-being. Once we were branded "Enemy Alien" and reduced to nothing more than "of the Japanese race," a phrase devised by the government, we were transfigured as scapegoats who would bear the mark of the enemy. [2, 3]

As far back as memory takes me, this mark was attached to the body, acting very much like a hovering shadow, *there* even when it was not apparent in consciousness. The shadow spread over the broader imagination of the events that dismantled the social, cultural, and economic fabric of ties *back* to the family homes in Haney, British Columbia, the small town in the lush, fruit-laden region of the Fraser Valley. In my young imagination, my family's expulsion from the West Coast meant that my own birth during their confinement in the site of relocation, Ste. Agathe, a small French-Canadian town not far from Winnipeg, must constitute a form of exile. Such a condition spawned an often-aching sense of absences—of a much richer and grounded home site *back there*, of closely knit community ties *back there*, and of a nurturing geography *back there*. Always *back there*. These absences were made tangible in memories of lost family photo albums, stored in a trunk with other memorabilia to be saved by neighbours, only to be sold off for a pittance at one of many government-sponsored public auctions. The few photos that were kept for the trip across country, as mementoes of what was left behind, became haunting icons of pre-internment life. It was the aura of estrangement from the past that shaped my childhood memory of the inner streets of Winnipeg where I grew up in the postwar years. Nowhere was this more palpable, at least to my young ears, than in one story, a bona fide ghost story, my father, Kazuo, told me many times.

Kazuo was born in BC in 1906 and grew up in *Nihon machi* (or "Japantown"), the area around Powell and Alexander Streets in Vancouver, where the majority of JCs in the city lived prior to the mass uprooting. One dark and stormy summer evening—yes, it had to be dark and stormy—a friend from the Fraser Valley, who couldn't return home, decided to stay at a Powell Street hotel. All the rooms were booked except for the one that was normally left empty. Rumours circulated in the community that it was haunted by a young woman murdered by her lover. Not superstitious at all, in fact, scoffing at the belief in ghosts, my father's friend rented the room. Well, not unexpectedly, since this was a ghost story, he was awakened in the middle of the night by moaning sounds. There in the smoked glass of the door appeared the figure of a woman with long black hair crying out to him for help. When the figure disappeared, he fled the hotel. The kicker, my father said, and this has always stuck with me, the ghost disappeared with the community when *Nihon machi* was dismantled in the mass uprooting in 1942. The story stuck with me so closely that my own version of it came to me in a poem, first written in the early 1970s. It invoked the figure of an old woman who used to wander the streets and back lanes of our central Winnipeg neighbourhood. She constantly talked to herself in

Japanese, and in her rambling speech she was always hunting for signposts of her lost Vancouver community. Like the ghost in my father's story, she became a manifestation of the internal effects of internment. I had recently moved to Vancouver, and as I wandered the Powell Street area, as I often did at the time, she appeared in my imagination, for me a premonition of the redress movement on the horizon—a movement that, in many ways, was driven by the desire to mediate a past haunted by the unacknowledged traumas of internment.

It is not surprising that, at first, many JCs shied away from public meetings on redress. There was the anxiety of being visible, of being perceived as other, and even of a racist backlash. Redress awakened memories of a past that had not been put to rest. When their surfaces were rubbed, even in casual conversations, individuals relived the scenes of uprooting, confinement, and suffering; once again unable to mediate the violations they had endured. They had learned that to be JC was to inhabit a consciousness that was divided by an internal contradiction: while "Canadian" signified the security of citizenship rights, national belonging, and democratic forms of governance, "Japanese" conjured the ghost of Enemy Alien, an identity that had condemned them to the dark underside of the nation—where they had been deprived of voice and the power to defend themselves.

Although government authorities, including the RCMP and the military, knew from evidence that the mass uprooting was not a necessary security measure, and that it reflected a capitulation to racist pressures in BC, decades had passed and nothing official had been done to acknowledge the injustices. Without such public recognition, JCs continued to bear the stigma of being identified as Enemy Alien. Having undergone the pressure to assimilate—to become the model minority—they still carried deep inside them the emotional and psychic haunting of internment. But how to move from here to there—from the condition of haunting to the House of Commons, the inner sanctum of the nation's power?

By using the *War Measures Act* to intern JCs, the government could argue as administrators and politicians did that it acted legally. Consequently, when the National Association of Japanese Canadians (NAJC) initiated redress as a political movement, they based their call for justice on the abuse of the *War Measures Act*. In other words, the government's policies may have been legal, but the effects of these policies—mass uprooting, dispossession, forced dispersal, and deportation—far exceeded the norms of fairness and due process under the law. The violation of citizenship rights on the basis of ascribed racial origin—being categorized as "of the Japanese race"—could not be defended as a necessary security measure.

Designing the call for redress would involve urgent questions of narrative, voice, and position, all the elements that required a careful attention to the language of redress. Shaping these elements took over two years, as the NAJC worked to bring together a fragmented group of JCs, who lacked knowledge of political movements and who had to struggle against the temptation to remain silent. But more, the role of "victim," often raised in the context of redress, especially by the national media, was rejected by many JCs. While they held the government accountable for their losses, they remained proud of the ways in which they managed to rebuild their lives and to maintain their loyalty to the Canadian nation. Their belief in democratic principles explains why the language of citizenship struck such a resonant chord for them, confirming as it did their efforts over many decades to be responsible Canadians. The abrogation of their rights, especially for the *Nisei* (second generation) in Canada, signified the ultimate insult to their faith in democracy. This attitude became a critical component of the case for redress presented in the NAJC's 1984 brief to the federal government. Instead of adopting the voice of victims who sought compensation for losses and damages (the language of law), the brief focused primarily on the democratic system itself. When the government wrongfully interned JCs, it argued, the principles of democratic governance were "betrayed" in its actions. *Democracy Betrayed: The Case for Redress*, the key document that propelled the NAJC's redress movement into the area of national politics, was released in Ottawa on 21 November 1984.[4]

The redress settlement may have been a political end to a long struggle for justice, but it was also the very medium through which a painful past could be transformed. Redress dominated my daily life for nearly a decade, drawing me into a relentless schedule of meetings, talks, lobbying sessions, and trips all over Canada. At times, the endless attention it required was all so overwhelming that the threat of pessimism and failure—of a collapse into cynicism—was never far away. But deeply immersed in the struggle, perhaps because of this, there were the more poetic moments—those astonishing moments when a turn would occur to reveal one of the signposts on what eventually became an unfolding path towards the settlement. My old friend, the poet bpNichol, who died suddenly and unexpectedly just days following the redress settlement, often talked about the need to "trust in the process" to get us through a creative negotiation with form. Maintaining a belief in redress called for this same trust in process and a respect for what it would conjure at the most unexpected occasions. I'll draw from three poetic moments of many; these are ones of extraordinary significance because they occurred during the summer of 1984, a period when the national redress movement took on a shape of its own.

One

The summer of 1984 was a volatile time for redress. An all-party government report on the effects of racism in Canada called *Equality Now!* had been issued with a recommendation in favour of a redress settlement,[5] but the Liberal government of Pierre Eliot Trudeau, and especially Trudeau himself, aggressively ruled out both an official acknowledgement of injustices and direct compensation. The most his government would offer was a statement of "regret" for what happened to JCs and a few million dollars to set up a vaguely described institute to commemorate their internment. At this same time, the talk of redress was creating waves within JC communities, and debates suddenly became strained in the face of Trudeau's rejection. Those of us trying to mount a redress movement in Vancouver decided to hold a public event on the evening before the large Powell Street Festival in Vancouver, the annual JC celebration held in Oppenheimer Park, set in the heart of what was once *Nihon machi*. Because of the reluctance of many senior JCs to be visible in public events, we knew that it was important to feature prominent speakers. Luckily, three speakers with large public profiles quickly said yes: David Suzuki, CBC broadcaster and scientist, Joy Kogawa, author of *Obasan*,[6] and Ann Sunahara, author of *The Politics of Racism: The Uprooting of Japanese Canadians during the Second World War*.[7] The only voice missing, at least from our perspective, was that of Tom Shoyama, one of the most well-regarded Nisei in the community. Shoyama had been the editor of *The New Canadian*,[8] the only community newspaper allowed to publish during the internment. In the postwar years, Shoyama garnered a national reputation as an influential organizer with Tommy Douglas's CCF (Cooperative Commonwealth Federal) party in Saskatchewan, and when he moved into federal politics he rose to become the deputy minister of finance under Liberal MP John Turner. Rumours were that Shoyama wanted to distance himself from the redress issue and, even more critically, did not support individual compensation. He had not responded to our invitation to speak at the event.

I was in Ottawa, more specifically at the Ottawa airport, on my way back home after a redress meeting, and worrying because we had not heard from Shoyama. If only I could talk with him face to face, so I thought, I could convince him to attend. As a highly respected Nisei, there was no doubt in my mind that his appearance would encourage many of his generation to attend. I had my head down, jotting down some notes for the conference, but then I glanced up and across the large waiting area of the airport. There, seated in the distance was a slender built man with a gentle face who looked like a JC. Tom Shoyama, I thought, could it be him? Could it actually be the one person I wanted to speak to at this very moment? I walked over to him and asked, "Tom Shoyama?" He smiled and nodded yes. After introducing myself as a coordinator for the conference, he politely said no thanks to the invitation. As a last resort I proposed that we sit together for the short flight from Ottawa to Toronto, his destination, and that if he felt the same way when we landed, I would respect his decision. He agreed, and luckily the flight was not full so we were able to sit beside each other. By the time we landed, he agreed to be our keynote speaker— and then off he went for another meeting of the Macdonald Commission on the economy, of which he was a member. At the public event, which filled to capacity (and more) inside the old Japanese Language Hall on Alexander Street, Shoyama publicly came out in favour of redress.

Two

That same summer the national political world was rife with anticipation, as John Turner replaced Trudeau, and all of the federal parties began campaigning for the September election. The NAJC was preparing a redress brief to submit to the political party that formed the next government. I was part of the brief writing committee, and given my background in academic research, I was asked to visit the national archives in Ottawa to make sure that our references to historic documents were accurate.

On the plane to Ottawa, I was busily working my way through one of the numerous drafts, noting which documents had to be located in which of the enormous number of files on internment that were housed at the national archives. While doing so, I was drawn from time to time into a conversation with a passenger next to me. As he picked up bits and pieces of what I was planning to do in Ottawa, he became more and more curious about the notion of redress and the brief we intended to submit to the federal government. He queried me about the mass uprooting, the destruction of the West Coast communities, and the confiscation of properties and belongings. He had grown up in the Maritimes, he said, and had little knowledge of the internment, but he expressed enthusiasm for the current decision to redress that past. I was in the process of pondering, yet again, the power of one BC politician in the cabinet of the Liberal government of Mackenzie King. Ian Mackenzie, a Vancouver MP, was perhaps the most vocal anti-JC voice in politics at the time, and his animosity evoked fear and anxiety among all JCs. Mackenzie campaigned stridently to expel them from BC, and they knew that in Ottawa his influence, as chair of the cabinet committee deciding on what to do about their presence on the west coast, had led directly to their mass uprooting and dispossession. It was Mackenzie whose campaign slogan was "Not a single Japanese from the Rockies to the sea!"[9] We cited his slogan in our redress brief, one of the most memorable of racist statements that were etched in the memories of JCs. Landing time came, and as we said our goodbyes my fellow passenger said that he would be watching for news about the progress of the movement. When we shook hands, he said his name was Ian Mackenzie—and then, as quickly as a moment passing, he blended into the crowd of departing passengers.

Three

On the last day of the parliamentary session, just before the campaign period began, Opposition leader Brian Mulroney challenged Trudeau's dismissal of redress. His voice rising in signs of anger, Trudeau once again declared that his government was not accountable for the past injustices endured by JCs. It was then that Mulroney declared that a Conservative government would "compensate" JCs, a statement that would be used in the four years ahead during which the NAJC would lobby his government. No one then expected the powerful Liberal machinery under Trudeau's leadership to crumble, but crumble it did by the time that John Turner took over as leader. In his brief public statements on redress, Turner revealed some distancing from the inflexible stance of Trudeau, though he did not make any commitments towards redress.

Turner's popularity was so unstable that his Liberal team decided that he should not take the chance of losing in Ontario and, instead, should run in the safest Liberal riding in Vancouver, the Point Grey riding of Quadra. The NAJC had not been able get close to Turner, but I thought that if we could simply talk to him we could get him to say his Liberal government would reconsider the question of redress. This is as much as we could expect, given Trudeau's response on behalf of the Liberal government.

I was sitting in our kitchen in our West 15th residence wondering what kind of strategy might work when I glanced outside to see a large bus coming slowly down the street. No doubt about it, the logo on its side boldly announced that the Liberal campaign was in full throttle in our neighbourhood. I quickly called my wife, Slavia, and my two kids, Waylen and Elisse, and then, just adjacent to our house, there was the man himself, John Turner, stepping down from the bus. I grabbed my camera and we all ran outside.

Looking somewhat haggard and drained of energy, Turner still remained upbeat, acting the role of the consummate politician. I thanked him half-jokingly for taking the time to visit me to talk about redress, and he smiled back in good humour. Surprisingly he seemed familiar with my work on the issue. We would wish him well, I said, if he would promise to keep the issue open after the election. He nodded, acknowledging that the issue was important to him, which for me was a positive-enough reply that the NAJC could use to continue lobbying for him in Ottawa. Turner would be elected in Quadra, but his party would suffer a devastating blow in the elections, losing 107 seats—from 147 to 40—in the House of Commons to a triumphant Conservative party. In the years ahead, when he assumed the role of Opposition leader, to his credit Turner consistently maintained support for a negotiated settlement with the NAJC. We marked the auspicious moment the Prime Minister paid us a visit by having his aide take a family photo with him—and then, as quickly as he arrived, off he went down the street with his liberal entourage.

Notes

1 Miki, Roy (2004). *Redress: Inside the Japanese Canadian Call for Justice*. Vancouver, BC: Raincoast Books.

2 Wood, S.T. (1942, February 7). A Public Notice by the Commissioner of the Royal Canadian Mounted Police Addressed to Male Enemy Aliens. Retrieved 2 November 2010 from: http://www.najc .ca/thenandnow/experiencec _firstorder.php

3 St. Laurent, L.S. (1942, February 26). A public notice by the Minister of Justice addressed to all persons of Japanese racial origin. Retrieved 2 November 2010 from: http://www.najc.ca/thenandnow/ experiencec_removal.php

4 National Association of Japanese Canadians (1984). *Democracy Betrayed: The Case for Redress*. A Submission to the Government of Canada on the Violation of Rights and Freedoms of Japanese Canadians during and after World War II. Winnipeg, MB: National Association of Japanese Canadians.

5 Special Committee on Visible Minorities in Canadian Society (1984). *Equality Now! Report of the Special Committee on Visible Minorities in Canadian Society*. Ottawa, ON: Queen's Printer. Bob Daudlin served as Committee Chair.

6 Kogawa, Joy (1981). *Obasan*. Toronto, ON: Penguin Canada.

7 Sunahara, A. Gomer (2000). *The Politics of Racism: The Uprooting of Japanese Canadians During the Second World War*. (2nd ed.). Ottawa, ON: Ann Gomer Sunahara. Retrieved 26 November 2010 from: http://www.japanesecanadian history.ca/index.html

8 *The New Canadian,* an English-only newspaper that was billed as the voice of the Nisei, began publishing in 1938 in Vancouver. Tom Shoyama took over as English editor from the original editor, Peter Higashi, in 1939.

9 Dyer, J. (1944, September 19). 'No Japs for B.C.' Mackenzie's pledge. *The Vancouver Sun*: 19.

Biography

Vancouver writer, poet, and editor **Roy Miki** taught in the English Department at Simon Fraser University from the mid-1970s until his retirement in 2007. He was a specialist in North American modernist and contemporary literature, and his teaching and research focused on the critical and creative implications of anti-racist theory, cultural studies, poetics, Canadian literature, minority literature, and Asian Canadian cultural production. A *sansei* (third generation) Japanese Canadian, Roy was born in Winnipeg in 1942 only months after his family was forcibly moved to Ste. Agathe, Manitoba, from their home in Haney, British Columbia. They were directly affected by the government's wartime decision to uproot, dispossess, and intern Japanese Canadians living on the West Coast of British Columbia. This cataclysmic event shaped Roy's formative years as an intellectual and as a writer. In the 1980s, as one of the spokespersons for the Japanese Canadian redress movement, he served on the Strategy Committee of the National Association of Japanese Canadians (NAJC), the organization that negotiated the historic redress settlement with the Canadian government on 22 September 1988. He has written numerous articles on redress as well as two books: with Cassandra Kobayashi, *Justice in Our Time: The Japanese Canadian Redress Movement*, a history of the NAJC's movement (NAJC/Talonbooks, 1991) and, more recently, *Redress: Inside the Japanese Canadian Call for Justice* (Raincoast, 2004), a work that blends archival sources, personal history, interviews, and critical commentary. Roy has also published four books of poetry, *Saving Face* (Turnstone, 1991), *Random Access File* (Red Deer Press, 1994), *Surrender* (Mercury, 2001), and *There* (New Star Books, 2006), as well as *Broken Entries* (Mercury, 1998), a collection of critical essays that examine race issues, writing, and subjectivity. *Surrender* was selected for the 2002 Governor General's Award for poetry. As an editor he has published work by bpNichol, George Bowering, and

Roy K. Kiyooka. His most recent edited work is Kiyooka's *The Artist and the Moose: A Fable of Forget* (LineBooks, 2009). Three books are forthcoming: *Mannequin Rising* (New Star Books), a book of poems, *In Flux: Transnational Signs of Asian Canadian Writing* (NeWest Press), a collection of essays, and *Dolphins' SOS* (Tradewind Books), a children's story written in collaboration with his wife Slavia Miki. Roy received the Order of Canada in 2006 and the Order of British Columbia in 2009.

Sisters outside the Pukatawagan day school with a group of boys
wearing Plains Indian-style headdresses made from paper, circa 1960
Attributed to sister Liliane
National Archives of Canada, PA-195120
[Reprinted from the Legacy of Hope Foundation's *Where Are the
Children?* exhibit catalogue (2003)]

Mike DeGagné

"I'm Sorry"

It is said we live in the Age of Apology. Governments and other public entities have discovered the wisdom of Apology, presuming that saying the right words has the power to heal. It allows those offering Apology to stand in a spotlight of grace and dignity.

Do we invest as much time considering how Apology is received? How do recipients hear, feel, and use Apology to restore what was lost?

For public institutions, Apology represents the triumph of empathy and understanding over cautious legal advice with an eye on liability. Some uplift us, others are shabby.

How do we measure Apology? Should we measure it at all? Is it important for Apology to be sincere, or is the act of Apology a form of penance?

We know when Apology is effective and when it misses the mark. It represents an opportunity to describe actions taken, and express our understanding of the harm that resulted. It is not always the best way to describe motives: "I chose an action, you were harmed, but I didn't mean it." Or worse still, "I meant well." At the heart of Apology is an understanding of the harm caused and its impact: "I harmed you. I understand that it left

you diminished in many ways. And it resulted in real consequences in your life."

The Indian Residential School System left a legacy in the
Aboriginal community that is real and present. Canadian society
often views this legacy as actions taken in the distant past, but
Survivors of these institutions carry the burden of this system
and its abuses even today. In recent decades we have seen churches, governments, public institutions, and individuals apologize
and express regret for the Indian Residential School System.
These apologies, some of which are presented here, convey an
understanding of the impact of historic trauma on Aboriginal
society decades later.

When reading these apologies, you are invited to reflect on a
few critical points:

Who delivered the Apology?

Does the Apology convey an understanding of the real
impact of harms done?

Does the Apology re-establish the victim's power by asking for forgiveness?

The real power of Apology comes afterwards, in the actions
taken to set things right. Many apologies allude to "taking a
different course in the future," but for governments, institutions,
and even churches this can be a difficult path. In the end the
impact of Apology may be reflected in forgiveness and what
remains on the hearts of those who receive them.

Learning from the Past
Documents of Reconciliation and Apology from Canadian Government and Churches

Editors' note: The following section presents a selection of Canadian Government and Church documents of apology to Aboriginal, Inuit, and Métis peoples for Indian Residential Schools. For a more complete collection of Apology documents, see *Response, Responsibility, and Renewal: Canada's Truth and Reconciliation Journey,* Volume 2 of Aboriginal Healing Foundation Research Series, edited by Marlene Brant Castellano, Linda Archibald, and Mike DeGagné.

For digital versions of these and other texts from the AHF Research Series, please visit http://speakingmytruth.ca.

Government of Canada "Statement of Reconciliation"

Jane Stewart, Minister of Indian Affairs and Northern Development, January 7, 1998

As Aboriginal and non-Aboriginal Canadians seek to move forward together in a process of renewal, it is essential that we deal with the legacies of the past affecting the Aboriginal peoples of Canada, including the First Nations, Inuit and Métis. Our purpose is not to rewrite history but, rather, to learn from our past and to find ways to deal with the negative impacts that certain historical decisions continue to have in our society today.

The ancestors of First Nations, Inuit and Métis peoples lived on this continent long before explorers from other continents first came to North America. For thousands of years before this country was founded, they enjoyed their own forms of government. Diverse, vibrant Aboriginal nations had ways of life rooted in fundamental values concerning their relationships to the Creator, the environment, and each other, in the role of Elders as the living memory of their ancestors, and in their responsibilities as custodians of the lands, waters and resources of their homelands.

The assistance and spiritual values of the Aboriginal peoples who welcomed the newcomers to this continent too often have been forgotten. The contributions made by all Aboriginal peoples to Canada's development, and the contributions that they continue to make to our society today, have not been properly acknowledged. The Government of Canada today, on behalf of all Canadians, acknowledges those contributions.

Sadly, our history with respect to the treatment of Aboriginal people is not something in which we can take pride. Attitudes of racial and cultural superiority led to a suppression of Aboriginal culture and values. As a country, we are burdened by past actions that resulted in weakening the identity of Aboriginal peoples, suppressing their languages and cultures, and outlawing spiritual practices. We must recognize the impact of these actions on the once self-sustaining nations that were disaggregated, disrupted, limited or even destroyed by the dispossession of traditional territory, by the relocation of Aboriginal people, and by some provisions of the Indian Act. We must acknowledge that the result of these actions was the erosion of the political, economic and social systems of Aboriginal people and nations.

Against the backdrop of these historical legacies, it is a remarkable tribute to the strength and endurance of Aboriginal people that they have maintained their historic diversity and identity. The Government of Canada today formally expresses to all Aboriginal people in Canada our profound regret for past actions of the federal government which have contributed to these difficult pages in the history of our relationship together.

One aspect of our relationship with Aboriginal people over this period that requires particular attention is the Residential School system. This system separated many children from their families and communities and prevented them from speaking their own languages and from learning about their heritage and cultures. In the worst cases, it left legacies of personal pain and distress that continue to reverberate in Aboriginal communities to this day. Tragically, some children were the victims of physical and sexual abuse.

The Government of Canada acknowledges the role it played in the development and administration of these schools. Particularly to those individuals who experienced the tragedy of sexual and physical abuse at residential schools, and who have carried this burden believing that in some way they must be responsible, we wish to emphasize that what you experienced was not your fault and should never have happened. To those of you who suffered this tragedy at residential schools, we are deeply sorry.

In dealing with the legacies of the Residential School system, the Government of Canada proposes to work with First Nations, Inuit and Métis people, the Churches and other interested parties to resolve the longstanding issues that must be addressed. We need to work together on a healing strategy to assist individuals and communities in dealing with the consequences of this sad era of our history.

No attempt at reconciliation with Aboriginal people can be complete without reference to the sad events culminating in the death of Métis leader Louis Riel. These events cannot be undone; however, we can and will continue to look for ways of affirming the contributions of Métis people in Canada and of reflecting Louis Riel's proper place in Canada's history.

Reconciliation is an ongoing process. In renewing our partnership, we must ensure that the mistakes which marked our past relationship are not repeated. The Government of Canada recognizes that policies that sought to assimilate Aboriginal people, women and men, were not the way to build a strong country. We must instead continue to find ways in which Aboriginal people can participate fully in the economic, political, cultural and social life of Canada in a manner which preserves and enhances the collective identities of Aboriginal communities, and allows them to evolve and flourish in the future. Working together to achieve our shared goals will benefit all Canadians, Aboriginal and non-Aboriginal alike.

Retrieved 13 Jan. 2012: http://www.aadnc-aandc.gc.ca/eng/1100100015725

Prime Minister Harper's "Apology on behalf of Canadians for the Indian Residential Schools system"

[On 11 June 2008, Canadian Prime Minister Stephen Harper offered a full apology on behalf of Canadians for the Indian Residential Schools system. Below is the text of his speech delivered in the House of Commons.]

The treatment of children in Indian Residential Schools is a sad chapter in our history.

For more than a century, Indian Residential Schools separated over 150,000 Aboriginal children from their families and communities. In the 1870's, the federal government, partly in order to meet its obligation to educate Aboriginal children, began to play a role in the development and administration of these schools. Two primary objectives of the Residential Schools system were to remove and isolate children from the influence of their homes, families, traditions and cultures, and to assimilate them into the dominant culture. These objectives were based on the assumption Aboriginal cultures and spiritual beliefs were inferior and unequal. Indeed, some sought, as it was infamously said, "to kill the Indian in the child". Today, we recognize that this policy of assimilation was wrong, has caused great harm, and has no place in our country.

One hundred and thirty-two federally-supported schools were located in every province and territory, except Newfoundland, New Brunswick and Prince Edward Island. Most schools were operated as "joint ventures" with Anglican, Catholic, Presbyterian or United Churches. The Government of Canada built an educational system in which very young children were often forcibly removed from their homes, often taken far from their communities. Many were inadequately fed, clothed and housed. All were deprived of the care and nurturing of their parents, grandparents and communities. First Nations, Inuit and Métis languages and cultural practices were prohibited in these schools. Tragically, some of these children died while attending residential schools and others never returned home.

The government now recognizes that the consequences of the Indian Residential Schools policy were profoundly negative and that this policy has had a lasting and damaging impact on Aboriginal culture, heritage and language. While some former students have spoken positively about their experiences at residential schools, these stories are far overshadowed by tragic accounts of the emotional, physical and sexual abuse and neglect of helpless children, and their separation from powerless families and communities.

The legacy of Indian Residential Schools has contributed to social problems that continue to exist in many communities today.

It has taken extraordinary courage for the thousands of survivors that have come forward to speak publicly about the abuse they suffered. It is a testament to their resilience as individuals and to the strength of their cultures. Regrettably, many former students are not with us today and died never having received a full apology from the Government of Canada.

The government recognizes that the absence of an apology has been an impediment to healing and reconciliation. Therefore, on behalf of the Government of Canada and all Canadians, I stand before you, in this Chamber so central to our life as a country, to apologize to Aboriginal Peoples for Canada's role in the Indian Residential Schools system.

To the approximately 80,000 living former students, and all family members and communities, the Government of Canada now recognizes that it was wrong to forcibly remove children from their homes and we apologize for having done this. We now recognize that it was wrong to separate children from rich and vibrant cultures and traditions that it created a void in many lives and communities, and we apologize for having done this. We now recognize that, in separating children from their families, we undermined the ability of many to adequately parent their own children and sowed the seeds for generations to follow, and we apologize for having done this. We now recognize that, far too often, these institutions gave rise to abuse or neglect and were inadequately controlled, and we apologize for failing to protect you. Not only did you suffer these abuses as children, but as you became parents, you were powerless to protect your own children from suffering the same experience, and for this we are sorry.

The burden of this experience has been on your shoulders for far too long. The burden is properly ours as a Government, and as a country. There is no place in Canada for the attitudes that inspired the Indian Residential Schools system to ever prevail again. You have been working on recovering from this experience for a long time and in a very real sense, we are now joining you on this journey. The Government of Canada sincerely apologizes and asks the forgiveness of the Aboriginal Peoples of this country for failing them so profoundly.

Nous le regrettons

We are sorry

Nimitataynan

Niminchinowesamin

Mamiattugut

In moving towards healing, reconciliation and resolution of the sad legacy of Indian Residential Schools, implementation of the Indian Residential Schools Settlement Agreement began on September 19, 2007. Years of work by survivors, communities, and Aboriginal organizations culminated in an agreement that gives us a new beginning and an opportunity to move forward together in partnership.

A cornerstone of the Settlement Agreement is the Indian Residential Schools Truth and Reconciliation Commission. This Commission presents a unique opportunity to educate all Canadians on the Indian Residential Schools system. It will be a positive step in forging a new relationship between Aboriginal Peoples and other Canadians, a relationship based on the knowledge of our shared history, a respect for each other and a desire to move forward together with a renewed understanding that strong families, strong communities and vibrant cultures and traditions will contribute to a stronger Canada for all of us.

Retrieved 24 November 2008 from: http://pm.gc.ca/eng/media.asp?id=2149

The United Church of Canada Apology to First Nations Peoples (1986)

Long before my people journeyed to this land your people were here, and you received from your Elders an understanding of creation and of the Mystery that surrounds us all that was deep, and rich, and to be treasured.

We did not hear you when you shared your vision. In our zeal to tell you of the good news of Jesus Christ we were closed to the value of your spirituality.

We confused Western ways and culture with the depth and breadth and length and height of the gospel of Christ. We imposed our civilization as a condition for accepting the gospel.

We tried to make you be like us and in so doing we helped to destroy the vision that made you what you were. As a result you, and we, are poorer and the image of the Creator in us is twisted, blurred, and we are not what we are meant by God to be.

We ask you to forgive us and to walk together with us in the Spirit of Christ so that our Peoples may be blessed and God's creation healed.

Right Reverend Robert Smith

Retrieved 26 November 2008 from: http://www.united-church.ca/beliefs/policies/1986/a651

The Missionary Oblates of Mary Immaculate:
An Apology to the First Nations of Canada by The Oblate Conference of Canada

The Missionary Oblates of Mary Immaculate in Canada wish, after one hundred and fifty years of being with and ministering to the Native Peoples of Canada, to offer an apology for certain aspects of that presence and ministry.

A number of historical circumstances make this moment in history most opportune for this.

First, there is a symbolic reason. Next year, 1992, marks the five hundredth anniversary of the arrival of Europeans on the shores of America. As large scale celebrations are being prepared to mark this occasion, the Oblates of Canada wish, through this apology, to show solidarity with many Native people in Canada whose history has been adversely affected by this event. Anthropological and sociological insights of the late 20th century have shown how deep, unchallenged, and damaging was the naive cultural, ethnic, linguistic, and religious superiority complex of Christian Europe when its Peoples met and interrelated with the aboriginal Peoples of North America.

As well, recent criticisms of Indian residential schools and the exposure of instances of physical and sexual abuse within these schools call for such an apology.

Given this history, Native Peoples and other groups alike are realizing that a certain healing needs to take place before a new and more truly cooperative phase of history can occur. This healing cannot however happen until some very complex, long-standing, and deep historical issues have been addressed.

It is in this context, and with a renewed pledge to be in solidarity with Native Peoples in a common struggle for justice, that we, the Oblates of Canada, offer this apology:

We apologize for the part we played in the cultural, ethnic, linguistic, and religious imperialism that was part of the mentality with which the Peoples of Europe first met the aboriginal Peoples and which consistently has lurked behind the way the Native Peoples of Canada have been treated by civil governments and by the churches. We were, naively, part of this mentality and were, in fact, often a key player in its implementation. We recognize that this mentality has, from the beginning, and ever since, continually threatened the cultural, linguistic, and religious traditions of the Native Peoples.

We recognize that many of the problems that beset Native communities today - high unemployment, alcoholism, family breakdown, domestic violence, spiraling suicide rates, lack of healthy self-esteem - are not so much the result of personal failure as they are the result of centuries of systemic imperialism. Any people stripped of its traditions as well as of its pride falls victim to precisely these social ills. For the part that we played, however inadvertent and naive that participation, might have been, in the setting up and maintaining of a system that stripped others of not only their lands but also of their cultural, linguistic, and religious traditions we sincerely apologize.

Beyond this regret for having been part of a system which, because of its historical privilege and assumed superiority did great damage to the Native Peoples of Canada, we wish to apologize more specifically for the following:

In sympathy with recent criticisms of Native Residential Schools, we wish to apologize for the part we played in the setting up and the maintaining of those schools. We apologize for the **existence of the schools themselves**, recognizing that the biggest abuse was not what happened in the schools, but that the schools themselves happened ... that the primal bond inherent within families was violated as a matter of policy, that children were usurped from their natural communities, and that, implicitly and explicitly, these schools operated out of the premise that European languages, traditions, and religious practices were superior to Native languages, traditions, and religious practices. The residential schools were an attempt to assimilate aboriginal Peoples and we played an important role in the unfolding of this design. For this we sincerely apologize.

We wish to apologize in a very particular way for the instances of physical and sexual abuse that occurred in those schools. We reiterate that the bigger issue of abuse was the existence of the schools themselves but we wish to publicly acknowledge that there were instances of individual physical and sexual abuse. Far from attempting to defend or rationalize these cases of abuse in any way, we wish to state publicly that we acknowledge that they were inexcusable, intolerable, and a betrayal of trust in one of its most serious forms. We deeply, and very specifically, apologize to every victim of such abuse and we seek help in searching for means to bring about healing.

Finally, we wish to apologize as well for our past dismissal of many of the riches of Native religious tradition. We broke some of your peace pipes, and we considered some of your sacred practices as pagan and superstitious. This too had its origins in the colonial mentality, our European superiorly complex, which was grounded in a particular view of history. We apologize for this blindness and disrespect.

One qualification is, however, in order. As we publicly acknowledge a certain blindness in our past, we wish, too, to publicly point to some of the salient reasons for this. We do this, not as a way of subtly excusing ourselves or of rationalizing in any way so as to denigrate this apology, but as a way of more fully exposing the reasons for our past blindness and, especially, as a way of honoring, despite their mistakes, those many men and women, Native and white alike, who gave their lives and their very blood in a dedication that was most sincere and heroic.

Hindsight makes for 20-20 vision and judging the past from the insights of the present is an exact and often cruel science. When Christopher Columbus set sail for the Americas, with the blessing of the Christian Church, Western civilization lacked the insights it needed to appreciate what Columbus met upon the shores of America. The cultural, linguistic, and ethical traditions of Europe were caught up in the naive belief that they were inherently superior to those found in other parts of the world. Without excusing this superiority complex, it is necessary to name it. Sincerity alone does not set people above their place in history.

Thousands of persons operated out of this mentality and gave their lives in dedication to an ideal that, while sincere in its intent, was, at one point, naively linked to a certain cultural, religious, linguistic, and ethnic superiority complex. These men and women sincerely believed that their vocations and actions were serving both God and the best interests of the Native Peoples to whom they were ministering. History has, partially, rendered a cruel judgment on their efforts, showing how, despite much sincerity and genuine dedication, their actions were sometimes naive and disrespectful in that they violated the sacred and cherished traditions of others. Hence, even as we apologize for some of the effects of their actions, we want at the same time to affirm their sincerity, the goodness of their intent, and the goodness, in many cases, of their actions.

Recognizing that within every sincere apology there is implicit the promise of conversion to a new way of acting. We, the Oblates of Canada, wish to pledge ourselves to a renewed relationship with Native Peoples which, while very much in line with the sincerity and intent of our past relationship, seeks to move beyond past mistakes to a new level of respect and mutuality. Hence ...

We renew the commitment we made 150 years ago to work with and for Native Peoples. In the spirit of our founder, Blessed Eugene De Mazenod, and the many dedicated missionaries who have served in Native communities during these 150 years, we again pledge to Native Peoples our service. We ask help in more judiciously discerning what forms that service might take today.

More specifically, we pledge ourselves to the following:

- We want to support an effective process of disclosure visa-vis Residential Schools. We offer to collaborate in any way we can so that the full story of the Indian Residential Schools may be written, that their positive and negative features may be recognized, and that an effective healing process might take place.

- We want to proclaim as inviolable the natural rights of Indian families, parents and children, so that never again will Indian communities and Indian parents see their children forcibly removed from them by other authorities.

- We want to denounce imperialism in all its forms and, concomitantly, pledge ourselves to work with Native Peoples in their efforts to recover their lands, their languages, their sacred traditions, and their rightful pride.

- We want, as Oblates, to meet with Native Peoples and together help forge a template for a renewed covenant of solidarity. Despite past mistakes and many present tensions, the Oblates have felt all along as if the Native Peoples and we belonged to the same family. As members of the same family it is imperative that we come again to that deep trust and solidarity that constitutes family. We recognize that the road beyond past hurt may be long and steep but we pledge ourselves anew to journey with Native Peoples on that road.

Reverend Doug Crosby

OMI President of the Oblate Conference of Canada

On behalf of the 1200 Missionary Oblates of Mary Immaculate living and ministering in Canada

Retrieved 25 November 2008 from: http://www.cccb.ca/site/images/stories/pdf/oblate_apology_english.pdfThe Anglican Church of Canada

A message from the Primate, Archbishop Michael Peers, to the National Native Convocation Minaki, Ontario

Friday, August 6, 1993

My Brothers and Sisters:

Together here with you I have listened as you have told your stories of the residential schools. I have heard the voices that have spoken of pain and hurt experienced in the schools, and of the scars which endure to this day.

I have felt shame and humiliation as I have heard of suffering inflicted by my people, and as I think of the part our church played in that suffering.

I am deeply conscious of the sacredness of the stories that you have told and I hold in the highest honour those who have told them.

I have heard with admiration the stories of people and communities who have worked at healing, and I am aware of how much healing is needed.

I also know that I am in need of healing, and my own people are in need of healing, and our church is in need of healing. Without that healing, we will continue the same attitudes that have done such damage in the past.

I also know that healing takes a long time, both for people and for communities.

I also know that it is God who heals, and that God can begin to heal when we open ourselves, our wounds, our failures and our shame to God. I want to take one step along that path here and now.

I accept and I confess before God and you, our failures in the residential schools. We failed you. We failed ourselves. We failed God. I am sorry, more than I can say, that we were part of a system which took you and your children from home and family.

I am sorry, more than I can say, that we tried to remake you in our image, taking from you your language and the signs of your identity.

I am sorry, more than I can say, that in our schools so many were abused physically, sexually, culturally and emotionally.

On behalf of the Anglican Church of Canada, I present our apology.

I do this at the desire of those in the Church like the National Executive Council, who know some of your stories and have asked me to apologize.

I do this in the name of many who do not know these stories.

And I do this even though there are those in the church who cannot accept the fact that these things were done in our name.

As soon as I am home, I shall tell all the bishops what I have said, and ask them to co-operate with me and with the National Executive Council in helping this healing at the local level. Some bishops have already begun this work.

I know how often you have heard words which have been empty because they have not been accompanied by actions. I pledge to you my best efforts, and the efforts of our church at the national level, to walk with you along the path of God's healing.

The work of the Residential Schools Working Group, the video, the commitment and the effort of the Special Assistants to the Primate for this work, the grants available for healing conferences, are some signs of that pledge, and we shall work for others.

This is Friday, the day of Jesus' suffering and death. It is the anniversary of the first atomic bomb at Hiroshima, one of the most terrible injuries ever inflicted by one people on another.

But even atomic bombs and Good Friday are not the last word. God raised Jesus from the dead as a sign that life and wholeness are the everlasting and unquenchable purpose of God.

Thank you for listening to me.

Michael Peers, Archbishop and Primate

Retrieved 11 November 2008 from: http://www.anglican.ca/Residential-Schools/resources/apology.htm

The Presbyterian Church in Canada: Confessions and Apologies

"It is with deep humility and in great sorrow that we come before God and our Aboriginal brothers and sisters with our confession..."

Our Confession:

The Holy Spirit, speaking in and through Scripture, calls The Presbyterian Church in Canada to confession. This confession is our response to the word of God. We understand our mission and ministry in new ways, in part because of the testimony of Aboriginal Peoples.

We, the 120th General Assembly of The Presbyterian Church in Canada, seeking the guidance of the Spirit of God, and aware of our own sin and shortcomings, are called to speak to the Church we love. We do this, out of new understandings of our past, not out of any sense of being superior to those who have gone before us, nor out of any sense that we would have done things differently in the same context. It is with deep humility and in great sorrow that we come before God and our Aboriginal brothers and sisters with our confession.

We acknowledge that the stated policy of the Government of Canada was to assimilate Aboriginal Peoples to the dominant culture, and that The Presbyterian Church in Canada co-operated in this policy. We acknowledge that the roots of the harm we have done are found in the attitudes and values of western European colonialism, and the assumption that what was not yet molded in our image was to be discovered and exploited. As part of that policy we, with other churches, encouraged the Government to ban some important spiritual practices through which Aboriginal Peoples experienced the presence of the creator God. For the Church's complicity in this policy we ask forgiveness.

We recognize that there were many members of The Presbyterian Church in Canada who, in good faith, gave unstintingly of themselves in love and compassion for their aboriginal brothers and sisters. We acknowledge their devotion and commend them for their work. We recognize that there were some who, with prophetic insight, were aware of the damage that was being done and protested, but their efforts were thwarted. We acknowledge their insight. For the times we did not support them adequately nor hear their cries for justice, we ask forgiveness.

We confess that The Presbyterian Church in Canada presumed to know better than Aboriginal Peoples what was needed for life. The Church said of our Aboriginal brothers and sisters, "If they could be like us, if they could think like us, talk like us, worship like us, sing like us, work like us, they would know God as we know God and therefore would have life abundant". In our cultural arrogance we have been blind to the ways in which our own understanding of the Gospel has been culturally conditioned, and because of our insensitivity to aboriginal cultures, we have demanded more of Aboriginal Peoples than the gospel requires, and have thus misrepresented Jesus Christ who loves all Peoples with compassionate, suffering love that all may come to God through him. For the Church's presumption we ask forgiveness.

We confess that, with the encouragement and assistance of the Government of Canada, The Presbyterian Church in Canada agreed to take the children of Aboriginal Peoples from their own homes and place them in Residential Schools. In these schools, children were deprived of their traditional ways, which were replaced with Euro-Canadian customs that were helpful in the process of assimilation. To carry out this process, The Presbyterian Church in Canada used disciplinary practices which were foreign to Aboriginal Peoples, and open to exploitation in physical and psychological punishment beyond any Christian maxim of care and discipline. In a setting of obedience and acquiescence there was opportunity for sexual abuse, and some were so abused. The effect of all this, for Aboriginal Peoples, was the loss of cultural identity and the loss of a secure sense of self. For the Church's insensitivity we ask forgiveness.

We regret that there are those whose lives have been deeply scarred by the effects of the mission and ministry of The Presbyterian Church in Canada. For our Church we ask forgiveness of God. It is our prayer that God, who is merciful, will guide us in compassionate ways towards helping them to heal.

We ask, also, for forgiveness from Aboriginal Peoples. What we have heard we acknowledge. It is our hope that those whom we have wronged with a hurt too deep for telling will accept what we have to say. With God's guidance our Church will seek opportunities to walk with Aboriginal Peoples to find healing and wholeness together as God's people.

"God not only calls the church to confession, but to a ministry of reconciliation, walking together, seeking to restore justice in relationships where it is lacking. Our church is called to commit itself to support processes for healing of the wounds inflicted on aboriginal people."

Retrieved 25 November 2008 from: http://www.presbyterian.ca/ministry/ canada/nativeministries/confessions

Glen Lowry

By Design: One Book, Among Many

Books are strange objects. Some people talk about books as machines, and there is something to be said for the idea of the pocket book as the prototypical mobile device—powerful, portable, popular. Others think of books as architecture: metaphoric warehouses, prisons, or playgrounds. There is no doubt that books, sometimes a single book, can be many things to many people. In fact, I might argue that the power of books rests in the complex social engagements they engender and reflect. As meeting places, spaces of assembly, the best books have an amazing ability to reach across expanses of time and space and to transform (themselves, us) in ways unimagined in the initial acts of writing or publishing.

When I was invited into the Aboriginal Healing Foundation's (AHF) Truth and Reconciliation Research Series (from which the texts of *Speaking My Truth* have been selected), I was brought in as a designer. I was tasked with thinking about the form of the third volume in the series, *Cultivating Canada*. I had to devise an approach that would represent the interplay between image and text, artworks and commentary. More than this, I needed to find an approach that could speak of and to the fraught history and memories of the Residential School System. Little did I know this would be the beginning of a much a longer journey. Little did I realize that taking on this design project would become a point of entry into a much larger and more powerful healing process—my own, among others.

Work on *Cultivating Canada* spread to include a redesign of the three-volume Truth and Reconciliation Research Series for a box set, then a book-club version of *Speaking My Truth* with translations in French and Inuktitut, a website, and now this new scholastic reprint of *Speaking My Truth*, in print and electronic versions. In the process, I found myself involved in a network of connections and interactions that have helped me reposition my work as a scholar, writer, editor, and publisher and to better understand the relationships between these modalities of practice.

This expanding web of AHF projects—a collection of texts and contexts that seems to morph as I type—has offered me the good fortune of participating in a vibrant, vital assembly of people and ideas. It has both enabled and challenged me to radically reconsider the way I understand literature and my role in teaching, learning and producing it. As an English scholar and teacher of Canadian literature, I came to the larger AHF research project burdened with knowledge that books can and have been violently misused. As a post-colonialist, I recognize that literature has been made to do the work of empire and nation, colonizing the minds of young and not-so-young readers. I remember that the study of literature—whether Shakespeare, Arnold, or Atwood—can be used as a blunt instrument to beat readers into submission.

These misgivings are highlighted when I think of artist-curator Jeff Thomas's multi-faceted exhibition *Where are the Children* (Legacy of Hope Foundation). Thomas provides viewers with an exacting presentation from the archival records of Residential Schools. Selected photographs show glimpses of Aboriginal, Inuit and Métis students learning to read and write. These images remind us that, in context of the Residential School System, literacy played a crucial role in a larger assimilationist project, in which children were forced by teachers, administrators, staff, clergy and laity to give up their language and traditional teachings for English instruction. The photographs of boys and girls sitting in rows rehearsing the alphabet or a line of prose, a few of which are reproduced in this volume, suggest a powerful perversion of the educational experience. They remind us—educators and students—of our privilege and ethical imperative.

Among the devastating materials included in Thomas's exhibition, those I find the most difficult to process are sample texts from the teachers' manuals and reports. These texts hinge on the language of "civilization" and "progress" and help describe the systematic brutality of Canada's colonizing approach to the children of Aboriginal, Inuit, and Métis communities across the country. Statements outlining the assimilationist goals of educators and ministries—their perceived or predicted successes— suggest the way that a single-minded approach to teaching and learning can be used to obliterate others ways of knowing.

Despite this undeniably violent history, despite the colonial function of the Canadian school system, in which literature and literacy played a crucial role, *Speaking My Truth* stands as a remarkable testament to the power of Survivors and the wealth of their stories. The power and generosity of these writers is not to be underestimated. Their ability to share the disturbing experiences of suffering and abuse alongside invaluable teachings on how and why they continue to find strength remain inspirational.

Stopping between chapters to take a breath and to reflect on the strength of the individual voices collected here, the material object of the book gives me hope. As I bend back the spine, thumb the pages, circle phrases, I feel a physical connection to the writers and readers who share these words. As my copy of this text takes on the marks of a living reading, I imagine how the language presented here has found its way back into the archive and has already begun to rewrite and reclaim teaching and learning as positive, community forming acts.

I look forward to hearing from new generations of readers and to learning how you carry these important ideas with you.